Praise for

# Postville, U.S.A.

" **T**HIS IS A BOOK THAT HAD TO BE WRITTEN, and Mark
Grey and his colleagues are the right people—perhaps
the only people—to write it. The story of Postville—its small
triumphs and failures and its one big disaster—is a made-
for-the-movies drama. The authors have spent months and
years in Postville. They've painted the broad story of the
drama, and they've also captured the nuances that the TV
cameras missed. Anyone who wants to understand immigra
tion and diversity—and needs to understand that they aren't
necessarily the same thing—must read this book. So must
those who think this nation can survive without immigrants, and those who think any of this will be easy.
Postville, U.S.A. is both a great yarn and a signpost to the
American future."

RICHARD C. LONGWORTH
*Caught in the Middle: America's Heartland in the Age of
Globalism*

Senior Fellow, Chicago Council on Global Affairs
Former senior correspondent, *Chicago Tribune* and
United Press International

"My parents are from small town Iowa, so I've seen the rapid demographic changes that have transformed some parts of this "American Gothic" landscape, as elsewhere. This book is an important close-up look at how the global economy, US labor policy, and a dysfunctional immigration system— forces beyond any city council's control—have buffeted one community, and how residents drew on traditional Midwestern tolerance to accommodate this change."

JENNIFER LUDDEN
Winner of the Robert F. Kennedy Award and the Society of Professional Journalists' Award for Excellence in Journalism

"This fresh, thoughtful take on Postville shows a town crushed by greed, federal indifference and a badly flawed immigration system, all fueled by America's demand for cheap food. It is a sobering read."

SUE FISHKOFF
The Rebbe's Army: Inside the World of Chabad-Lubavitch and Kosher Nation, (forthcoming) on kashrut and kosher food production.

*"Postville has been called an inflection point in America's immigration debate and the most egregious case of abusive interventionism in decades. This book offers a timely inside portrait of the town, its background, struggles, and hopes. The authors' longtime, intimate local knowledge makes this an invaluable historical document. Their subject matter expertise as social scientists makes it a piercing wake-up call to our nation and generation."*

ERIK CAMAYD-FREIXAS

Professor, Florida International University; Federal Court Interpreter; and Co-Author, *Postville: La Criminalización De Los Migrantes* [*Postville: Criminalization of the Migrants*]

*"In* Postville, U.S.A.: Surviving Diversity in Small-Town America *Mark Grey, Michele Devlin and Aaron Goldsmith expose the absurdity of destroying a small town in the name of enforcing archaic immigration laws. Does anyone believe the ICE raid on Postville really accomplished anything? But* Postville, U.S.A. *is more than just the story of a tragedy. It's a testament to one small Iowa community's citizens' refusal to let adversity destroy their town.*

Postville, U.S.A. *is a must read for anyone concerned about America's illegal immigration problem and the obvious lack of solutions."*

BOB BRUCE
*The Bob Bruce Radio Experience*
600 WMT, Cedar Rapids, Iowa

# Postville, U.S.A.

# Postville, U.S.A.

## Surviving Diversity in Small-Town America

Mark A. Grey

Michele Devlin

and Aaron Goldsmith

GEMMA

Boston

POSTVILLE, U.S.A: Surviving Diversity in Small-Town
America

First published by GemmaMedia in 2009.

GemmaMedia
230 Commercial Street
Boston MA 02109 USA
617 938 9833
www.gemmamedia.com

Printed in the United States of America

Cover design by Night & Day Design

12 11 10 09 08 1 2 3 4 5

ISBN: 978-1-934848-64-7

Library of Congress Preassigned Control Number (PCN)
applied for

*From Mark to Mary, Megan, and Julia Cameron*

*From Michele to Daniel, Tim, Alli, Carol, and Jack*

*From Aaron to his wife, Esther Miriam; his children,
Yitzy, Mimi, Shmuly, Chani, Shuky, Moishy, and
Rochel; his mother and father; his sister, Bryna; Rabbi
Y. Newman; and his friends Chani, Chaim, and Hall*

*From all of us to the good people of Postville*

# CONTENTS

# Contents

# FOREWORD

D RIVE EAST ON HIGHWAY 18 in Iowa long enough, past the rolling hills of corn and soybeans, and you'll come to Postville, Hometown to the World. It's an impressive, urban-sounding slogan for a town with no stoplight. Keep traveling past the rows of big leafy trees shading open-air porches built a century ago, and you'll come to the closest thing you'll find to a traffic jam: the four-way stop at Tilden and Lawler Streets. The next stoplight is in another town, miles and miles away, where one can also find a proper big-box retailer like Wal-Mart. Yet this intersection, with a Mexican restaurant, Jewish library and Somali grocery store represents the epicenter of a truly global society and economy.

Here in the most improbable of places, the abstract, sweeping themes of free market capitalism, religious politics and immigration policy intersect with cold, hard reality—the human drama that unfolds when people from thirty-five different countries converge on an isolated town of 2,000 people and decide to call each other "neighbor." I can't think of a grander, wilder social experiment. What emerges from this preposterous brew is not only a story of hope and beauty, but also of pain and devastation.

As towns across the country embark on the road toward ethnic diversification, Postville should serve both as a beacon of hope and an uncompromising cautionary tale. Postville's recent past will be rural America's future. If the lessons presented in this book aren't heeded, then Postville's fractured and fragile present could be the future of too many rural towns.

The story of Postville is one of the most nuanced, layered, and frankly, compelling stories in America. Part of Postville's magic is that everyone loves an underdog. As a journalist writing dozens of articles and conducting hundreds of interviews in Postville, it's still hard to believe these impossibly huge global themes all landed here, in the unlikeliest of places. It's no surprise then that it has drawn journalists from around the world, from the *New York Times* to an Academy Award-nominated Guatemalan filmmaker.

It has been a privilege to document this little town's happenings on a regular basis. Like any good story, it contains much laughter, but also many tears of sorrow. As the son of a recent Mexican immigrant, I take the Postville story to heart. I can also empathize with the difficulties that accompany conflicting languages and cultures in this tiny Iowa town. Only a few years into my career, I wonder if I'll ever stumble into a meatier assignment with so many serious implications for the future of our society.

What makes this book special are the years of sweat and tears Grey, Devlin and Goldsmith poured into the issue of trying to make multiculturalism work. To understand this interconnected world we live in, there's really only one option: extract yourself from the plush office chair in your air-conditioned office, and get your boots dirty. Then go home, wash up, and head right back into the grimy, dusty field, all the time thinking, 'You know, I really don't get paid enough for this.' In other words, be a good journalist. Of course, journalists like me have deadlines, write many stories every week, and have limited column inches to explain complex issues. With these restraints, we journalists can focus on only one aspect of the community at a time. It takes many resources, continuity and unique, in-depth knowledge to provide comprehensive perspective of a community over several years. In today's journalism world, devoting those kinds of resources to a small, isolated town like Postville is simply not an option.

But that's exactly what Grey, Devlin and Goldsmith have been doing for more than a decade. Out of their labor comes the gripping tale of a little town that stood tall in the face of incredible odds, only to find out that it was on the losing end of global forces bigger than itself and even its country.

Americans love to talk about the myth of the Melting Pot, but it is another thing to make it work. Americans also love to talk about the miracles diversity can bring, but only as long as it seems to benefit them as individuals and interest groups. Grey, Devlin and Goldsmith have exposed the various interests who have tried to make Postville what they thought it should be. And there certainly have been a lot of agendas for Postville—from the Neo-Nazis who use the "failure" of Postville to claim multicultural and multireligious communities can't work, to the Politically Correct who claimed Postville as long as it "worked" and could be held up as a model of Diversity.

As this book makes clear, the reality lies somewhere in between these disparate agendas. Making a multiethnic and multireligious area work is a difficult but potentially rewarding struggle that requires people to take ownership of their communities and define what success means to them.

Please consider this the definitive commentary on modern-day Postville, from the arrival of Agriprocessors to the immediate aftermath of the historic immigration raid on the kosher meatpacking plant. At its core, it is a tragic tale. "The Little Kosher Meatpacking Plant That Could" injected a stagnant town with incredible life and energy, only to throw it all away, taking the community down with it on its way to a spectacular fall.

But the story isn't over yet. Here's to Postville's resiliency and eventual success. All the world will be watching.

JENS MANUAL KROGSTAD
—*Award-winning author and multimedia journalist; Waterloo, Iowa.*

# INTRODUCTION

**W**HEN DEVELOPING A CREATIVE WORK such as a book, song, or poem about a beloved place or person, some writers sense that the story is already out there in the ether of life and they have only to intuitively receive the information and commit it to paper—almost as if an author is a radio, picking up a story as it floats through the airwaves. For solo authors it may be easy to get on the right frequency and separate the story from the noise. Only one radio is working at a time. But when there are two authors or, in our case, three authors, there are more radios, all tuned to different frequencies. Before we started this project, we all agreed there has been a story about the unique little town of Postville, Iowa but it took years for us to realize how our different experiences and perspectives on the community could mesh and form a common voice.

At times, collaborating on this book has felt like one of those jokes about disparate people thrown together, something like "an anthropologist, a minority public health expert, and a rabbi walk into a bar

. . . " Or "an Episcopalian, a Catholic, and a Jew walk into a bar . . . ." We have known each other for ten years and are well aware of our differences. But writing a book together has made us realize how many things we have in common, too. The most important of these is a genuine fascination with, love of, and belief in Postville. At times we almost felt that Postville was the center of the universe; there were forces at work in the spiritual and earthly world that seemed to converge in this tiny town in the middle of nowhere. Of all places on earth, how did Postville become so significant to our understanding of the human condition in the early 21st Century as the world faces increased globalization, migration, and rapidly changing ethnic diversity?

Writing a book is often a labor of love. Our book is the product of our affection for Postville and our belief that no matter how tarnished its reputation may be in the short term, its story holds great promise for the future of rural America.

Two of us, Mark and Michele, are professors, and we make a living in towns like Postville. We have done research and consulting in Postville's environs for more than ten years. Michele was trained as a refugee health specialist at UCLA, and Mark was trained in applied anthropology at the University of Colorado, Boulder. Both of us have worked extensively abroad and were on track to continue our global careers. We even wrote dissertations based upon research among Ethiopian refugee women and migrant workers in Southern Africa. When we both accepted faculty jobs in Iowa in the early 1990s, our timing could not have been more fortuitous. We arrived just as Postville and dozens of other rural Iowa towns started to experience big influxes of immigrants and refugees. The culture clash that resulted from rapid ethnic diversification presented tremendous challenges to schools, health-care providers, law enforcement, community leaders, and newcomers themselves. As administrators in centers at the University of Northern Iowa that address immigrant and refugee issues, we have been busy for years addressing the state's changing demographics through research, lecturing, and consulting with thousands of Iowans as they work through the challenges posed by our burgeoning newcomer populations. We were trained to go out into the world beyond the United States, but we didn't have to go anywhere: the world came to us.

Our third author, Aaron, lives and works in Postville. Aaron is a native Midwesterner who grew up in a Chicago suburb. He studied business at Drake University in Des Moines and then pursued rabbinical training in Israel. After serving for two years as a Jewish rabbi in Long Beach, California, Aaron became involved in a medical-equipment business. Although he eventually moved his business to Postville, his interest in moving to the town was more personal than professional: he and his family were drawn by Postville's thriving Hassidic community and Orthodox Jewish schools for his five children.

Even though we have lived in Iowa for many years, we all have relatives and friends who have never visited us here. Iowa is not a destination, in their opinion. It's a place you drive through or fly over on your way to someplace else. Michele grew up in Los Angeles. When she goes home, mentioning the fact she lives in Iowa is often met with howls of laughter and disbelief. To some of her acquaintances, she had moved to the dark side of the moon. Mark, who left Colorado, heard friends declare it would be difficult to remain close since he was moving to such a backward place. How could they take seriously anyone who would leave Boulder for *Iowa*? It was even worse for Aaron. When he moved his family from the West Coast to Iowa, some of his friends asked Aaron, "What is it like to fall off the end of the world?" Some were more blunt and offered to say Jewish *kaddish* prayers for him, which are typically recited for the recently deceased.

Some might think our cultural, religious, or gender differences make collaboration impossible. After all, very few Orthodox Jews coauthor books with Christians, and lay observers might not expect a gender-segregating Hassidic Jewish male to work with women, especially a non-Jewish one. But collaborate we did, and the book you are holding is proof that such a collaboration can work. How did we reach agreement on the complex issues at play in Postville? Well, we didn't always—but we did most of the time. And gradually we came to see our backgrounds and relationships as an apt microcosm of the complex interreligious and multiethnic relationships that typify Postville. We recognized that we had far more similarities than differences among us and that our divergent voices could ultimately combine into one as invested occupants of, and visitors to, this town.

This book could have been written any time in the last ten years, during which both national and international media have focused on Postville's remarkable move toward diversity. But writing it became imperative after the tremendous jolt Postville received in May 2008, when the Immigration and Customs Enforcement (ICE) raided the Agriprocessors kosher meatpacking plant. The raid itself, at that time the largest raid of a single-site employer in United States history, stripped the meat plant of most of its workforce and cut Postville's population by more than 20 percent. The ICE raid turned Postville from the poster child for diversity into the epicenter for our nation's ongoing debate about immigration and globalization.

Before the ICE raid, media attention focused on the arrival of Orthodox Jews in Postville and their relationship with local Christians. We focus on this relationship as well, and we benefit from Aaron's experience as a member of this Orthodox community and his status as a rabbi. However, we also recognize the roles of many other ethnic and religious populations that live in Postville. Our limited discussion of some of these groups, such as the Guatemalans arrested during the ICE raid, does not represent a lack of respect for these people or any population in Postville.

In examining what happened in Postville, we look closely at several issues: the rapidly changing demographics of rural America due to globalization and the migration of international laborers; the benefits and problems for host communities associated with these ethnic changes; the disturbing violation of worker rights and exploitation of vulnerable new-comers by some companies in the absence of immigration reform; and how politically correct "diversity" professionals and other outsiders with their own agendas for Postville imposed their own standards for success on the community, rather than encouraging the town itself to generate its own model for cultural tolerance and respect. This book is not just another voice in the often insincere debate over international migration, ethnic relations, and the "need for diversity." While these superficial discussions rage, the real world—places like Postville—gets on with the messy business of life through the often difficult but rewarding process of mutual accommodation.

Some in the media like to portray issues in cut-and-dried terms, and Postville is no exception. First it was a success story; then it became a failure. But the truth, of course, is far more complicated. As we hope to show in this book, complex, nuanced issues such as ethnic relations, cultural identity, and human migration are in no way simplified when they occur in a small town such as Postville. The town, like any, is a collection of human beings, all of whom bring their own agendas, priorities, experiences, and feelings to bear. Nothing is black and white.

Many of the people we encounter and the media have wanted an end to the story—a lesson learned, a curtain closed. But we contend the story is still in progress. Postville is still finding a way to make itself "work." What happened, and continues to happen, in Postville provides myriad lessons for the rest of the nation as we become increasingly multicultural and multiethnic. We all have to figure out how to make it work.

CHAPTER ONE

# Iowa and the New Demographics

AMERICANS LOVE THEIR STEREOTYPES about
Iowa. A state with endless miles of cornfields, all
those little towns, so quaint, so boring, so *white* . . .

Many people are so caught up in their own
urban-rural biases about Iowa that they refuse to believe that there is any ethnic diversity in the state—
let alone recognize that, in fact, the state has a strong
reputation for cultural tolerance and moderation.
Indeed, researchers, non-profit organizations, and
other human service providers that deal with multicultural issues are sometimes denied grants to meet
the needs of these diverse populations in the state because funders from metropolitan enclaves outside of
Iowa—who should know the new national demographic trends better—are skeptical that Iowa has
any minorities at all.

So, needless to say, many Americans have a hard
time believing that crucial battles about the future of

our society—the future of a multicultural America—are being played out in rural Iowa.

Iowa *is* an overwhelmingly white state. Today, more than 90 percent of the population is white. But that's changing, and quickly. The state is undergoing a fundamental shift that reflects demographic changes at the national level, and particularly those ethnic shifts that are now occurring in rural America. Since 1990 many Iowa communities have experienced "rapid ethnic diversification"—the transition from populations that are predominately or exclusively white and English-speaking to those that are multiethnic, multicultural and multilingual, all in the course of a few short years.

Most of Iowa's demographic changes are due to rapid growth in immigrant and refugee populations. The vast majority of newcomers are Latino immigrants from Mexico, drawn by jobs in meatpacking, construction, and hospitality. Iowa's Latino immigrants are among the fastest growing Latino populations of any state. But Iowa is also home to immigrants from such disparate places as the Congo, Somalia, Iran, Vietnam, Laos, Honduras, Guatemala, Bosnia, India, the former Soviet Union, Iraq, Burma, and the Central Pacific. Iowa's capital, Des Moines, has one of the largest concentrations of Sudanese refugees in the United States, second only to its Midwestern neighbor Omaha, Nebraska. The net result of rapid ethnic diversification is that Iowa today looks and feels very different from the Iowa that existed a mere twenty years ago. And stereotypes about "the heartland" don't fit anymore.

In 2008, the U.S. Census Bureau projected that by 2042 our country's nonwhites, taken as a group, will outnumber whites. Whites will no longer be the majority in our society. There are a number of reasons for this, including the aging of white baby boomers, higher birth rates among minorities, and immigration. Today, for every new white resident in the U.S., there are about eleven new nonwhite residents.

As a society we're still not sure what to call this phenomenon. Some use the awkward term "majority minority" to describe nonwhite populations that outnumber whites. We sometimes call it the "Anglo Inversion."

Nonwhites already form the majority in states such as Texas and California, and in major cities such as Washington, D.C. Iowa is not far behind. In some Iowa school districts, the total minority population outnumbers whites. In towns such as tiny Conesville, (pop. 424), in the eastern part of the state, more than half of the residents are now Latino.

Our nation has long looked to cities to instruct us about ethnic relations. We try to learn from the mistakes made and triumphs achieved in these huge cauldrons of ethnicity, religion, race, and class. The results have been mixed. Looking forward, we see dramatic growth in multiethnic suburbs. Do the lessons from the cities teach us how to make these new communities work? Or are we simply moving our urban issues to the land of strip malls? Can we apply the lessons learned by demographically altered cities and suburbs to rural American communities such as Postville, Iowa?

Many professional and lay observers of cities and suburbs ignore what's happening in rural communities. Despite their rapid influxes of immigrants, refugees, and other ethnically diverse populations, small towns don't have sufficiently large minority populations, and they lack the intense diversity of languages, cultures, and nationalities found in larger cities. So some believe. And so, to these minds, small towns don't merit attention.

The intense and immense mix of peoples in today's urban areas is sometimes referred to in Mexican slang as *menudo*, or tripe soup. A similar term in Yiddish is *cholent*, a kind of stew made with lots of pieces of foods—usually leftovers—that normally wouldn't be cooked together.

Well, there is plenty of *menudo* and *cholent* now in Iowa. The forces of class, race, ethnicity, and power, long at work in cities, also play themselves out in rural communities, often with some very serious implications for the future of our society. Indeed, these smaller communities can serve as unique social experiments in diversity exactly because there are fewer main players in this human drama, and the consequences of immigration policy, human actions, and the like can be followed and studied much more closely. It's time to get past talking about "diversity" and whether or not one community's "diversity" is more legitimate than another's. Indeed, it's time to also get past "valuing diversity" as a dodge when people don't really want to talk about difficult issues like class or personal political agendas. We will say a great deal more about the diversity business later, but for now suffice it to say that rural towns have generally not been granted legitimacy by diversity professionals because of their own stereotypes about rural enclaves or simply because there isn't a large enough market for the products or trainings they're promoting.

Diverse rural communities face another dilemma: many rural residents don't care much for or about cities (or suburbs), don't have a great deal of respect for urban problems, and don't see how the multicultural experience in, say, Los Angeles has any bearing on their lives. Cities are exactly what most rural Iowan communities do not want to become, even on a significantly smaller scale. Yet with the rapid growth of minority populations in small towns, the issues rural people believed were once confined to urban areas have now come to them. As some people put it, "those people" have arrived, bringing an urgent need for bilingual teachers, medical interpreters, training in ethnic relations for law enforcement officials, and the like.

But without "those people," many Iowa towns would be well down the road to extinction. The state's population has grown with immigration: two-thirds of Iowa's total growth since 1990 is due primarily to a significant influx of Latinos and other immigrants and refugees from around the world. Iowa is typical of rural farm states that are experiencing an exodus of young white people, declining birth rates, the concentration of new populations in urban areas, and an aging rural white population. Indeed, two-thirds of Iowa's ninety-nine counties experienced their peak populations before 1950, and half of them peaked prior to 1900. Over the last two decades, there have been three kinds of Iowa communities: urban areas such as Des Moines that have grown with relatively diverse economies and burgeoning suburbs; rural communities that are shrinking and aging rapidly; and towns that have grown with immigration.

Among the rural towns that have grown is little Postville, with a meager population of 2,273 residents in the year 2000. Postville was typical of rural farm towns in Iowa that saw their fortunes turn for the worse with the demise of the family farm in the 1980s and the loss of jobs in the local meatpacking plant. Between 1980 and 1990, the population barely changed, from 1,475 to 1,473.

But bucking the trend among most rural Iowa towns, Postville grew significantly in the 1990s and early 2000s. There were large influxes of immigrants and Orthodox Jews after the local meatpacking plant reopened as the nation's largest kosher meat producer. This plant, opened by the Rubashkin family of Crown Heights, New York, is named Agriprocessors. In many respects, Agriprocessors revitalized Postville, bringing hundreds of new jobs and a sizable payroll.

By attracting an ethnically diverse workforce, and helping to establish a large community of Orthodox or *Hassidic* Jews, the plant literally changed the face of Postville. The challenges and opportunities associated with these influxes of newcomers are a focus of our book.

When you drive into Postville, the welcome sign reads "Postville: Hometown to the World." It is apt.

Postville has experienced tremendous and rapid ethnic diversification; over the years the town has counted residents from more than fifty nations, and Postville schools enrolled students from thirty-five different countries. At times, Postville felt more like a huge metropolis than a rural town, so great was its variety of people, languages, cultures, and religions. Postville's Jewish grocery store has thirty-seven clocks on its wall. Each represents a time zone associated with Postville immigrants who have come and gone over the years. For such a small town, with a population peaked at a couple of thousand residents, the population diversity was remarkable.

With such tremendous diversity, Postville became a sort of experiment in social integration. Most of the media attention focused on the Jews in town, many of whom were deeply observant and kept to strict kosher lifestyles. The media portrayed them as determined to separate themselves from non-Jewish residents, but that was often exaggerated. For many of the Jews, their lives simply had a different rhythm from those of the Christian locals due to strict adherence to their religious obligations, including the daily cycle of prayer and observance of the Sabbath. But misrepresentations aside, the relationship between the Jews and Christian Postvillians is critical to understanding these groups' relationships with other newcomers to the town and Postville's integration as a whole.

Together, we three have lived or worked in Postville for many years. From Mark and Michele's research and activism there and Aaron's experience living and working in the town, we know the community very well and have written and spoken about its experiences in a variety of academic and non-academic settings. It is quite normal for any us to conduct a workshop or give a speech involving Postville. It is also quite normal to give our audiences the opportunity to ask questions. In true proper upper-Midwestern fashion, many of our audience members, though, will not ask a controversial question in public, and our attempts to engage them in debate about Postville can often fall silent. We can predict what will happen next, after the polite applause: People will line up and one-by-one step up to one of us, lean close to our ears and say, "I didn't want to ask this in front of the group, but . . . " And what do they ask most in these private moments? They usually ask some variation of the question, "Does Postville *really* work?" It's a fair question.

Diversity brought great things to Postville. A critical number of people worked hard to pull the community together and celebrate its cultural diversity. People from many cultures reached out to others, formed coalitions, addressed concerns, and organized events. We will say a good deal about these good efforts later. We admit that at times we thought Postville would be a national model for multicultural integration and not just another meatpacking town with problems such as high crime rates and social transience. At times we even felt that we were witnessing small miracles. There was, it seemed, something very special about Postville, something different. It was working.

We're convinced that, left to its own devices and with the sustained opportunity for all Postvillians to continue to create a community on their own terms, Postville would remain a model of multicultural accord. But it hasn't turned turn out that way. We had long ago considered writing a book about Postville, but now that we have, it's not the book any of us envisioned. Indeed, the lessons of Postville, so meaningful for rural America and our entire society in light of demographic change are principally not about the good work of well-meaning people but about the political and corporate forces that pounded Postville and ultimately led to its current challenges. The book we wanted to write, the book about idyllic Postville, the hometown to the world, has become a cautionary tale, but one still imbued with hope and opportunity.

# CHAPTER TWO

# Shtetl on the Great Plains

CROSS THE GREAT EXPANSE of the American Midwest, Postville is just a speck. Under normal circumstances, it wouldn't draw much attention. It's just another small Iowa town, founded some 150 years ago by European settlers. Postville was originally a German Lutheran community, and the place is still full of families with names like Schroeder, with the occasional Scandinavian Gunderson. Other than the water tower, the tallest structure in town is the steeple on St. Paul's Lutheran Church. The other established churches are Catholic and Presbyterian.

Postville is located in the rolling hills of northeastern Iowa. The colors of the surrounding landscape change with the seasons, from the rich, deep greens of spring after the corn sprouts, to the golden browns of fall and the harvest, to the bleak, white emptiness of winter. Postville's immediate setting is unremarkable, but it's surrounded by spectacular scenery. The Mississippi River is about half an hour away; the high bluffs that line the river in that part of Iowa offer some of the most beautiful vistas in the country. To the north and south of Postville lie deep valleys lined with spring-fed creeks, some filled with trout. Picturesque farms overlook the valleys, and dairy cattle graze the hillsides.

No Wal-Mart or McDonalds interrupts this idyll. These so-called outposts of civilization are twenty-five miles away in Decorah, an otherwise quaint college town. The nearest airport with scheduled service is more than an hour and a half away, in La Crosse, Wisconsin, though most Postvillians drive an extra half hour to the busier Cedar Rapids airport. Some even drive three and a half hours to Minneapolis to catch a direct flight.

In the entire town of Postville, you won't find a single stoplight. It doesn't need one. There's just one four-way stop, where U.S. Highways 52 and 18 head southeast toward the Mississippi River. When the siren goes off at the volunteer fire department, the police chief or one of his staff stands in the middle of the intersection of Greene and Tilden Streets to stop the grain trucks and other vehicles coming into town, clearing a path for the fire trucks.

On a pleasant day, it's not uncommon for people to walk the length and breadth of town. Nothing and no one is more than a few blocks away. Everyone seems to know where everyone else lives. Just like your typical small town.

In some ways, Postville also is a typical meatpacking town, dependent on the local packinghouse for its economic survival. Meatpacking plants, in turn, have developed a tremendous dependence on immigrant and refugee workers who are qualified for packing jobs precisely because they are unqualified for other employment. You don't need to speak English or have an advanced education or special job skills to cut up animals. You only need to be able-bodied and willing to do grueling work for meager wages. It is not so unusual, then, that Postville has experienced influxes of immigrants and refugees from around the world.

In the 1990s, they came from Mexico, the Ukraine, Russia, and dozens of other countries. Recently, most newcomers have come from Guatemala, Palau, and Somalia. Over the years, most workers have been Latino, but Postville also has temporarily hosted people from China and Pakistan. However, these workers and their families tend to come in waves, and long-term settlement is rare. Turnover rates in meatpacking plants are notoriously high—often reaching 80 percent or more per year—and that's been the case in the Postville plant. So, the immigrants come and go in spurts. Although the town has one of the smallest school districts in Iowa—the entire district fits into two buildings—Postville has enrolled students speaking more than seventeen different native languages.

While this level of ethnic diversity is not unusual in large cities, tiny Postville has faced significant challenges in meeting the needs of thousands of immigrants who have revolved in and out of the community over a relatively short period. Even before this influx, Postville was an underserved community in a resource-poor state. The town often faced shortages of doctors, teachers, and other vital personnel, and it had a very small tax base from which to operate. The steady flow of newcomers from around the world multiplied the community's basic needs and amplified its challenges.

Today, most consumers are generations removed from rural farm life and many barely consider that the chicken, turkey, beef, and other meat products they eat were once living animals. The vast majority of this livestock is slaughtered, gutted, skinned, plucked, chopped, or otherwise processed in rapid-fire, assembly-line fashion and often by immigrant labor. (The meatpacking industry refers to this process as the *dis*assembly line.) Killing and cutting up hundreds or even thousands of animals a day is ugly, bloody, physically demanding work.

The wages are too low to attract locals and in most cases, including Postville, the number of available workers is insufficient, regardless of wage levels. In Iowa, for instance, about half of the high school and college graduates leave for higher paying work in other states, and the remaining whites have fertility rates that are too low to replace these native emigrants. Also, like the American population as a whole, Iowa is aging dramatically and becoming more urban.

Meatpacking is also among the most dangerous occupations in the United States. Meatpacking plants are largely automated, but machines can't perform every task. Humans must do the rest.

Injuries are far too common; the list can include repetitive motion problems in joints, muscle strains from heavy lifting, lacerations from sharp blades, burns from cleaning chemicals, and hearing loss from noisy machines. In part, injury rates are so high in agricultural processing plants because profit margins are so low. To make larger profits, plants must slaughter more animals. That means working at speeds that are mind-numbing and dangerous.

Some plants don't offer health insurance. And even among those that do offer health benefits, workers may opt to buy insurance only for themselves, preferring to spend what little leftover salary they have on their family. Often, health insurance doesn't kick in until workers have been on the job for three to six months; unfortunately, it's during those early months that new workers are most likely to be severely injured due to their unfamiliarity with the job.

With these poor working conditions, high injury rates, few benefits, and low wages, it's no wonder turnover rates in the industry are tremendous. Some plants have reported aggregate rates over 100 percent. In one plant we observed, 25 percent of all workers had been on the job for less than a month. It's not unusual for new hires to walk out before the end of training—as soon as they understand the nature of the job.

Many immigrants and refugees take packing jobs because they aren't eligible for other jobs. And because so many are desperate for any kind of job, they're willing to work for lower wages than most local people. This is particularly true, of course, for those living and working in the United States without legal immigration papers.

In the old days, meatpacking plants in rural
Iowa—including the plant in Postville that shut down
and was eventually reopened as a kosher plant—were
unionized and paid working-class if not middle-class
wages. Turnover was virtually unheard of. Iowans
used to want these jobs. But the industry started to
change in the 1980s, with downward pressure on
wages, higher capacity and more efficient plants, and
the weakening of unions. Plants lost interest in hiring locals. Instead, the industry became deeply dependent on immigrants and other workers who were
unfamiliar with the old expectations for working
conditions and wages, and who were willing—often
out of desperation—to migrate to jobs in remote
rural American towns. This is exactly what happened
in Postville.

Our description of Postville can be used for dozens
of meatpacking towns in the Midwest. Postville had
an old-line beef packing plant for decades. It was a
Hygrade plant that hired locals and paid good wages,
and the workers enjoyed union representation. However, the older and smaller plant shut down in the
1980s, when it no longer could compete with much
larger plants that offered lower wages and economies
of scale. Another former plant in town, Iowa Turkey
Processors, employed 350 at its peak. About half of
these workers were immigrants from Mexico and
Eastern Europe. The first Latino workers in Postville
arrived about 1991 to work at the plant they called
"la Turkey." When the plant burned to the ground
on December 20, 2001, its owners chose to move its
operations to Minnesota. The turkey plant's closure

left 350 people unemployed, but many quickly migrated to work at the plant next door.

In 1987, the plant reopened as Agriprocessors, a kosher slaughterhouse. It became—and remained, until May 2008—the largest kosher packing plant in the country—some say in the world. Kosher products are those that have been prepared, processed, and packaged according to strict Jewish religious laws. Observant Jews consume kosher foods for religious purposes, and production of these goods is a highly lucrative niche market.

Agriprocessors—locals call it "Agri" for short, and Mexican workers call it "La Agri"—is owned and operated by an Orthodox Jewish family from Brooklyn who are members of the Chabad-Lubavitcher sect of Judaism. The plant's founder is Aaron Rubashkin, the family patriarch, who built a kosher meat empire from his small butcher shop in Crown Heights. For many years, Shalom, his son, served as vice president and ran the day-to-day operations of the plant. He was assisted on a daily basis by his brother, Heshy Rubashkin.

The Rubashkins opened a plant in Postville for several possible reasons. First, the former Hygrade packing plant was available at a reasonable cost, and it could be remodeled as a kosher facility. Second, the plant is in the middle of the U.S., with markets on the East and West coasts at roughly the same distance. Third, Iowa is a right-to-work state; workers don't have to join a union to work in an organized plant. The Rubashkins were eager to avoid unions in their facility. And fourth, by buying a plant in Iowa, the Rubashkins moved closer to the source of their raw material: livestock. Shalom Rubashkin once told the media, "How we wound up here [in Postville], who knows, but Iowa is where the cattle, turkeys, and chickens are grown." Further in the interview, he observed, "In New York City, you don't grow much good cattle." Despite the production of kosher meat, the Agri plant was established in the Midwest for the same reasons non-kosher plants are located here: this is where the cheap, highly subsidized corn and soybeans are grown to feed and fatten the livestock in wide open spaces in close proximity to the packing plants.

The Agri plant is best known for its specialized production of kosher meats under a variety of labels, such as Aaron's Best, Shor Habor and Supreme Kosher, although at one point in its history, two-thirds of its meat production was for non-kosher markets sold under other labels such as Iowa's Best Beef. By industry standards, Agri is a small plant and a small operation. A large, modern beef plant may slaughter and process a few thousand cows each day; at most, Agri slaughtered about 500 each day. Modern chicken plants slaughter several thousand chickens each hour; the Postville plant slaughtered 60,000 chickens over two shifts, fewer than a thousand each hour. There are two reasons for this. First, to produce meat that meets strict kosher certification, the animals must be killed by hand by specially trained rabbis. Cows' throats are slit with a long silver knife, and poultry is killed with knives roughly six inches long.

Killing by hand is a much slower process than methods used in plants with killing machines.

The other reason Agri has much smaller product turnover is that the kosher process is time and labor intensive At Agri, two kinds of inspectors work side by side: the United States Department of Agriculture inspectors and kosher supervisors called *mashgichim* from external kosher certification organizations like the Orthodox Union (OU), who must oversee every aspect of production. This not only slows things down but also greatly adds to production costs. Kosher meat also must be completely free of blood, adding more steps and expenses to the process. And all these additional processes require additional steps in treating the plant's waste water.

The Agri plant is also unique because it produces *Glatt* kosher beef. This meat comes from slaughtered cows that are inspected to meet the highest kosher standards. The cows must have smooth lungs containing no holes or other defects. Kosher supervisors use pressurized air to blow up the lungs from these cows' carcasses; if they don't leak, and if the cows meet other standards of purity, they may be certified as *Glatt* kosher.

Many books have been written about kosher food production under Jewish law, and we recognize our treatment of kosher is superficial and over simplified. Kosher food production is based on traditions and principles developed thousands of years ago, some dating back to the time of Moses. Perhaps most important for readers to understand is that kosher meat isn't simply meat that is "blessed" by a rabbi. It is the product of a complicated and time-consuming process. (Non-kosher meat is not wasted, of course, and meat that doesn't meet high kosher standards may still be accepted for sale in other markets operated under the less stringent standards of the United States Department of Agriculture.)

Kosher meat is much more expensive to produce than conventional meat, but because it sells at premium prices, the profit margins are higher, too. The primary markets for Agri products are the East Coast, Los Angeles, and other communities with high percentages of observant Jews. However, their products are distributed around the world to Jewish communities in Israel, South America, Europe, and other locations. Jews who want kosher meat produced under the strict laws of *Kashrut*, which governs their dietary life, are willing to pay much higher prices than they would pay for non-kosher meat. For years Agriprocessors had the biggest share, by far, of this lucrative market. In 2007, the company supplied 60 percent of the nation's kosher meat and 40 percent of its kosher poultry. One of the plant's main accomplishments was to provide access to kosher meat products in remote communities, where Jewish consumers previously had limited access to such goods.

Agriprocessors also began to penetrate lucrative non-Jewish markets, as more and more consumers demanded natural, organic, or minimally processed foods. These consumers, Jewish and non-Jewish alike, patronize trendy natural food stores such as Trader

Joe's in West Los Angeles and are as likely to be devoted buyers of high-priced kosher chicken breasts
produced by Agriprocessors as are Orthodox Jews
from neighborhood kosher delis. Indeed, 70 percent
of receipts at Agriprocessors have come from the sale
of non-kosher meat.

Because kosher meat must be produced under the
watchful eye of certified rabbis, Postville is home to
some 300 Hassidic (which means pious in English),
Orthodox Jews who fulfill specialized roles within
the plant, such as *shochtim*, or slaughterers. Postville
boasts the highest number of rabbis per capita in the
United States.

On a typical day in Postville, one can find people from many different parts of the world walking
the streets in traditional Orthodox Jewish garb, including the long black robes and distinctive hats of
the local Jewish residents who put Postville on the
map. On *Shabbat*, or the Sabbath, which starts on Friday evenings and ends on Saturday night, Jews are
forbidden to drive, so families walk through town on
their way to the synagogue. Long beards and hats
distinguish members of the different Jewish sects.
Followers of the Chabad-Lubavitch movement often
wear a traditional black, broad-rimmed fedora. Members of the *Sigit* movement wear large, saucer-shaped
fur hats that may be two feet wide and about six inches tall. Members of the *Belz* sect also wear fur hats, but
theirs look more like traditional Russian sable hats,
rising up to a foot above the wearer's head. There are
also members of the *Vizhnitz* movement, as well as

other Orthodox and even secular Jews who come from diverse locations, ranging from Brooklyn, New York and New Jersey to Russia, Argentina, Lithuania and Israel. Every day, observant Jewish men wear *kippas*, or skullcaps, in public as a sign of commitment to G—d. (Out of respect for the sacredness and holiness of the Divine Name, Orthodox Jews do not spell out the name of the Creator in writings. This lessens the chance of it being erased, destroyed, or discarded, even in languages other than Hebrew.) The Jewish married women dress modestly and generally wear wigs or scarves in public out of modesty.

Among Orthodox Jews, gender segregation starts at an early age. Jewish children start attending boys' or girls' schools when they are about four years old. Adult activities outside the home, including worship, parties, and work are generally segregated, too.

In Postville, Orthodox Jews also tend to segregate themselves from non-Jews, although the degree to which this happens is often exaggerated. The majority of Orthodox Jewish kids don't attend the public schools. But Jews and non-Jews are neighbors, and they often work together. All of Aaron's employees, as it happens, are non-Jewish men and women. Menachem Gabbay, the Orthodox owner of GAL Investments in Postville, also employed a number of white Christian Iowans and jokingly would refer to his head accountant as his "day wife." Granted, the Jews and non-Jews usually don't share active social lives, but on occasion some will attend each others' special holiday traditions, such as the festive community

Hanukkah celebration that was sponsored by the Jews for many years.

However, Orthodox Jews and non-Jews don't often share that most important generator of social bonding in small-town America: food. The Orthodox Jews live strict kosher lifestyles, including restrictions on what they may eat and drink and how their food is prepared. When Orthodox Jews and non-Jews do share food, the Jews generally provide it, and they prepare it in their own kosher kitchens or buy it at the local kosher market. There are exceptions, such as fruit and certain drinks that are certified kosher. (When some of the Postville Jews have eaten in our homes they usually bring their own prepared food, eat off of plastic disposable plates, or consume only naturally kosher foods like fruit and vegetables.) Observant Jews have kosher kitchens with, for example, separate sinks for washing plates and pans that have come into contact with meat or dairy products. Non-Jews tend to not have kosher kitchens, of course, or pay particular attention to whether the food they buy is kosher, so Orthodox Jews can't consume their food.

For some, language represents another built-in segregator. Some adult Jews in Postville speak only Yiddish or Hebrew. Some of the Jews are from Israel, Eastern Europe, or South America, while many others are born-and-bred Americans from states such as New York and California.

The Jews in Postville have long captivated the curiosity of a number of local Iowans, particularly those in nearby small towns who, perhaps, never interact-

ed with anyone other than Christians during their up-
bringing. In the United States, which has the largest
concentration of Jews in the world (nearly 6,000,000),
most Jews practice Reform or Conservative Judaism.
Relatively few are Orthodox Hassidic Jews, like those
in Postville. Some Iowans likened these Jews to the
Amish, another unique ethnic group in Iowa, because
of their deeply conservative religious customs and traditional dress codes. Outside Postville, Iowans also
tended to assume the Orthodox Jews are all alike, and
they were lumped into a nebulous group called "the
Jews." Many outsiders were oblivious to the sharp lin-
guistic, religious, cultural, and ethnic differences between the various Jewish sects. Whether they were
Israeli or American, secular or Orthodox, rich or poor,
they risked being seen as a single group. For example,
Agriprocessors was a privately owned family business
run by the Rubashkins, and many of the Jewish workers were contracted slaughters from a firm in New
York and unrelated to the family. Still, both groups
were frequently mistaken as the same by external observers, the media and residents alike, and "The Jews"
tended to be collectively held responsible for the rise
or fall of Postville.

With the establishment and growth of the Agri
plant, Postville experienced growth in the number of
rabbis (Jewish scholars), many of whom had specialized vocational training in the highly ritualistic tech-
niques of kosher hand slaughtering (*shochet*). These
rabbis were often young, and most had large families
with seemingly ever-increasing numbers of children.
As their numbers grew, so did their need for the spe-

cial infrastructure it takes to support an Orthodox Jewish community. First was the synagogue, built in and around a large old farmhouse on the southern end of town, about one block south of the Lutheran Church. Then the preschool and segregated schools for younger boys and girls, which were established by Leah Rubashkin, wife of the kosher plant's founding manager, Shalom. (Aaron moved his family to Postville largely because of the availability of schooling for his five children.) In time, they also built *mikvahs* (ritual bath houses) for men and women. The Rubashkins opened a kosher market and restaurant to support the dietary needs of the Jewish population. Orthodox Jews established a *yeshiva*, or seminary for young Jewish men who are learning the Torah and other sacred scriptures. Today, Jewish families from throughout North America send their sons to Postville for rabbinical education in an idyllic, isolated, rural setting relatively free of big-city temptations and distractions.

A few years ago, the Jewish community opened the Northeast Iowa Judaic Resource Center and Library in town. Operated by the devoted, gracious Rabbi Aaron Schimmel, this center is a central library for Jewish texts and educational programs. It also serves as an outreach center for the non-Jewish population. As members of Chabad, Rabbi Schimmel and his eager young yeshiva volunteers often spent their time giving tours to curious groups of Christian university professors and foreign exchange students or demonstrating the proper way to light menorahs or build ritual huts for the fall holiday of *Sukkhot* for even more curious secular Jews in nearby Waterloo, Iowa.

The size of this tight-knit Jewish population and its well-developed infrastructure led some Jews in town to refer to Postville as a shtetl. Shtetl is a Yiddish term that literally means "little town." Shtetls (the plural in Yiddish is *shtetlekh*) were small towns with large Jewish populations that existed throughout pre-Holocaust Eastern and Central Europe. Some shtetls were founded a thousand years ago. Shtetls were socially stable and resilient communities where Orthodox Judaism flourished, safe from outside influence or interference.

Most of the Orthodox sects represented in Postville have their roots in different shtetls. Members of the Lubavitch movement, for example, trace their roots to the Russian shtetl of Lubavitch, a Jewish community that started in the late eighteenth century.

Most Americans are familiar with the concept of shtetl through the play and movie *Fiddler on the Roof*, which portrayed the beauty and pain of the shtetl in Eastern Europe as it experienced periods of prosperity and tolerance and endured times of extreme poverty and pogroms. During the period depicted in the play, riots were directed at Jews and other groups; people were murdered, and homes, synagogues, and businesses destroyed. At times, the pogroms were carried out with the blessing of local governments.

Today, the term shtetl often is used as a metaphor for European Jewish life in the nineteenth century.

Many Jews in Postville refer to the town as a shtetl because of the relative physical isolation of the community, its integration with a predominately Christian town, and its well-established infrastructure. Some use the term when they feel threatened by outside influences and negative portrayals in the media. Some Israeli Jews, with a distinct preference for cosmopolitan urban living, use the word shtetl to describe small-town rural life. The term is so closely associated with Postville that Rabbi Schimmel is seeking the establishment of a kosher-related museum in Postville, highlighting the town's status as an American shtetl.

The establishment of a shtetl and the presence of so many Hassidic Jews in Postville have spawned a great deal of interest in the media. It is a fascinating and rather peculiar situation, and the curiosity is understandable. At times, tourists from as far away as Chicago, New York, and even Israel have wandered through the town to take photographs and wonder at this unique social experiment. Others have made documentaries, published stories, or written articles about this unique little town.

The earliest published reference we've found to modern Postville's unique ethnic mix is in a 1996 book entitled *Boychiks in the Hood: Travels in the Hasidic Underground*, by Robert Eisenberg. *Boychik* is Yiddish for "young man," and the title is a play on the name of the movie *Boyz in the Hood*. Eisenberg provides glimpses of Hassidic life in several locations around the world, in places like Boro Park, New York;

Domrova, Poland; and Los Angeles. His chapter on Postville is called "Lake Oybegone." Eisenberg seems both intrigued and put off by Postville's isolation, writing "if the Diaspora were the solar system, Postville would be Pluto." Yet he admires the Jews on the streets who look "like extras in a *Fiddler on the Roof* production," another reference to Postville as a shtetl.

Eisenberg recognized that the primary thing that brought so many Jews to such an isolated place was the money that could be made in the kosher meat business. He acknowledges, perhaps somewhat grudgingly, that even in Postville Jews can develop relations with *goyim* or non-Jews while also forming their own community. He admired the way Postville Jews lived and worshipped together: "It is a community in its truest sense and an absolute abnegation of the anomie and atomization so pervasive in the contemporary world. Even by the standards of other Hasidic communities, it is all very cozy, for there is nowhere else to go . . . . Yet there is no discernible disharmony, and they approach everything with the enthusiasm of a group of people spearheading a reconnaissance mission to the most distant outpost of the Diaspora to establish a Hasidic colony there."

Today Eisenberg may come across as a bit dreamy. But we must remember that he visited Postville in the early 1990s, only a few years after the Agri plant opened and Hassidic Jews began to arrive in Postville. At that time, many of the Jews no doubt felt as though they were establishing a Hassidic outpost at the far reaches of the Diaspora.

In 1998, National Public Radio brought the Postville story to a national audience. Jackie Northam, who later became NPR's correspondent at Guantanamo Bay, introduced her report by acknowledging that for most people, Iowa "conjures up images of wide open spaces and clean simple living rather than culture clashes and religious divisions." Northam described Postville, pre-Agriprocessors, as "something out of Norman Rockwell painting." Then, when the Rubashkins opened their kosher packing plant, the presence of so many Jews and rabbis made Postville look "less like a Norman Rockwell and more like a set from *Fiddler on the Roof.*" This didn't always go over well with the locals, she explained. At first, local Postvillians were bewildered by the Jew's clothing and put off by the Jews' desire to segregate themselves and their reluctance to share meals with neighbors. Locals wondered at their slow response to accept the Iowan cultural obligations of clearing snowy sidewalks and mowing lawns regularly. Other little things bothered the locals, too, like the newcomers' failure to wave hello to Gentile neighbors on the street or involve themselves in local events. But Northam reported that with time relations improved, and Jewish and non-Jewish neighbors began to have friendly exchanges. Even Shalom Rubashkin, who considered himself a diehard New Yorker, began to consider himself an Iowan, as Northam noted: "Ten years ago, he would never have believed that Lubavitcher Jews and Iowa farmers could live and work so closely together: 'This is an experiment that has worked and has shown that if people want to, they can do it . . . when you live in a small town like this, you need each other. And I say, we've learned to live with each other.'" Still, Northam closed her piece by suggesting that the Jews and the established residents in Postville lived side by side with the "resignation of an arranged marriage."

These themes have been repeated time and time again in coverage of Postville. The Iowa Public Television (IPTV) documentary "Postville: When Cultures Collide" took a similar view. For better or worse, this sixty-minute show, released in 2001 and the product of an unusually large budget and vast resources, has become standard fare in sociology, anthropology, religion, history, social work, and education classes around the United States. The Postville Jewish library keeps a copy to orient Jews and non-Jews to the town's history.

The video includes a combination of live shots of people living and work in Postville and an array of talking heads (including two of us.) The video's producers acknowledged that they were interested in Postville mainly because so many Hassidic Jews live there; it was only after some prompting by Mark and others that the film crew decided to include coverage of the town's rapidly growing Latino community. The video explains that Postville's Latino expanding population helped save the town's school system. As school enrollment grew, Postville bucked the trend in small towns by hiring rather than laying off teachers. The video's footage and narrative about the Latinos took some of the focus off the Jews and rounded out the story.

One of our old colleagues found the film offensive, because he felt it made fun of the "old timers" who were trying to maintain some sense of integrity in the community as they had known it their entire lives. In one particularly poignant moment some of the established Postvillians expressed their dismay at the Jew's insistence on gender segregation as the natives sat in the local café—men at one table and women at another.

But in the end, the video is about Jewish versus non-Jewish relations. The themes are predictable: the locals had a hard time with the social isolation of the Jews. "The Jews" didn't adhere to important local standards such as cutting their grass or driving slowly, and "the Jews" didn't always seem to have the best interests of Postville in mind. Still, the video's overriding message seems to be that although the change in Postville's makeup has been difficult, and there's no sense in *not* acknowledging the challenges, most people try to make Postville work to the best of their ability.

Perhaps one of the best known popular accounts of Postville was written by Stephen Bloom, the author of *Postville: A Clash of Cultures in Heartland America* (2000). Bloom is a journalist who moved with his family from San Francisco to Iowa City to take a faculty position at the University of Iowa. He identifies himself as someone who is not a "religious Jew." Bloom began to visit Postville in late 1990s, drawn by the presence of the Hassidim. "I wanted to understand why they were here. Had they decided that they could find a clear path to salvation in Iowa? . . .

I daydreamed that the Postville Jews would be long-lost relatives who had found us in this remote place in the corner of America."

Bloom's book provided an interesting treatise on his personal struggle with his Jewish identity and his cultural transition from urban California to rural Iowa. Because his book is accessible and well written, and because Bloom wrote it when there were no other meaningful books about Postville's unique community, it gained a wide readership outside Iowa. Bloom quickly was presumed to be an expert on rapid ethnic diversification in rural America, although it's an area removed from his training. He became the outside world's primary talking head and expert on Postville and remained so for almost a decade.

To some of Bloom's readers in the lucrative East and West Coast sales markets—many of whom may have had their own preconceived notions about life in the rural Midwest—the complex, multidimensional, and very human rural Iowans, Latino workers, Jews, and others about whom Bloom wrote seemed an unlikely cast of characters in a bizarre Hollywood script.

Nowhere is this oversimplification more evident than in the full-color photo collage the publisher developed for the cover of the book. It shows an Orthodox Jewish man with a long beard, long black gown, and a fur hat walking as he reads from a small religious text. He is on a sidewalk in front of five elderly white (probably Lutheran) male farmers, two of whom are wearing overalls, which are fairly uncommon attire in Iowa. One farmer is looking at the passing Jew with an expression of mild disdain or bewilderment. Neither of the two photos that make up this collage was taken in Postville, and both are highly idealized. For years, people visiting Postville brought along copies of the book and asked locals to show them where the photo was taken, only to be disappointed when they learned the scene did not exist.

Despite the book's popularity around the country (it even briefly made the *New York Times* bestseller list), many Postville residents argued that it did not portray their community accurately. Many Orthodox Jews saw it as a disdainful view of their conservative group by a liberal, secular Jew. Many of the local Christian Iowans in town felt they were made out to be backward country hicks. And many saw Bloom's perspectives on Postville more likely based on common urban-rural biases than on religious and class differences between the author and the town's inhabitants.

In the book, Bloom tries to make it clear that his experience in Postville did not match his expectations. Nonetheless, as we noted earlier, this professor of journalism, who came from California and lived hours away from Postville, became the media's primary commentator on the town. He was often expected to play the role of social scientist in areas outside his specialty, such as demographic change, human migration, and the impact of globalization on rural America.

Postville has moved on quite dramatically in the decade since Bloom studied it, and we have been working and living in Postville throughout this "post-Bloom" phase. The quaint and curious little town at the center of his storytelling has now attained a level of complexity, fascination, and relevance that Bloom could not have imagined when he left it years ago. That's one of the reasons we wrote this book. The significance of this tiny community has now grown out of proportion to its size. It has gone from being a minor cultural curiosity during Bloom's time to sitting center stage on the national and even international debate about immigration, a global economy, and migrant worker rights.

# CHAPTER THREE

# Small Miracles

W E HAVE GIVEN COUNTLESS public speeches, workshops, and other talks about Postville over the years. We've worked or lived in the community for a number of years and have watched the town go through all kinds of growing pains, tensions, crises, and triumphs of dignity. People who have read Bloom's book, seen the negative media coverage, or heard rumors about Postville often asked us some variation of the question "Does the town really work?"

Skeptics ask this question anticipating evidence to fit their expectation that such a polyglot and multiethnic community, and particularly one with so many Jews, is doomed. We recognize among some of these skeptics anti-Semites who express their biases with varying degrees of discretion. But many are biased against any of the newcomers, motivated by ethnocentric or racist sentiments.

At the other end of the spectrum of curious people, we encounter those who hope Postville works because they "believe in diversity." They tend to express some variation of the Rodney King appeal that we all should "get along." Human beings are, at base, good natured and capable of loving each other, despite differences in religion, language, culture and ethnicity. They want to feel about Postville as many of us do when we watch examples of universal goodwill during the Olympics.

Hardened realists though we are, at times we've felt Postville showed the world what can happen when radically diverse communities recognize that their differences are not as important as their commonalities. Sometimes we even believed we were witnessing small miracles.

Aaron's election to the Postville City Council was one such miracle. In December 2000, Aaron was appointed to fill out the term of a council member who had been elected to the Iowa Statehouse. It was a one-year appointment. The city council member who recommended Aaron, noted his success at running a local business, his participation in the Postville Chamber of Commerce, and his progressive attitude about Postville. "We just felt he was the man for it, and with all the Jews and Mexicans and Russians we have here, we've got to have some communication." Aaron didn't seek out the position, noting that Orthodox Jews generally don't run for public office. And it was not an objective of Postville's Jewish community to place a Jew on the city council. Still, he decided to accept the position out of a profound regard for the community. As a local business owner, he had a vested interest in the health of the town; as a citizen, he also cared deeply about its welfare.

Throughout the long history of Postville, no one had ever challenged an appointment to the city council, but this time someone did. The petitioner was Arlin Schager, a retired Postville resident. Schager called for a special election for Aaron's seat; his petition received enough signatures (126) to force the city council to set a special election for April 2001. But it became clear that several people signed the petition without fully understanding it and without realizing that the council had already appointed Aaron. The city clerk echoed these concerns, noting that a few signers came into city hall to withdraw their signatures after they understood the petition's full impact.

Why did Schager start the petition? He told the reporters, "We knew very little about Mr. Goldsmith. This is America, after all, and we have the right to have a say in our community." (In the afterword to the 2001 paperback version of his book, Bloom claimed that Schager "went so far as to predict that violence would erupt in Postville.") Some people who signed the petition were more direct, telling the press—under condition of anonymity—that they didn't want a Jew on the city council. One woman, who did give her name told the *Los Angeles Times*, "We're just afraid that if they get one in, then pretty soon the whole council will be Jewish, and they're going to run the town." Although Aaron didn't work at Agriprocessors, has no familial relationship to the Rubashkins, and is an American citizen, to this woman's mind he was one of "the Jews" certain to take over the community with ruinous consequences.

Schager stood his own daughter, Tracey, to run against Aaron. Although she clearly stated she was not motivated by anti-Semitism, the election ignited a firestorm of controversy and, of course, media interest. Print and electronic media from as far away as Scandinavia descended on Postville. At times, the town was clogged with TV satellite trucks. CNN referred to the situation as a setting for a "Hollywood sitcom" with a "comic premise." A television station from St. Paul called the election a challenge to Postville's "melting-pot status."

It was a spectacle, with hordes of media following Aaron and his challenger around town. The more media, the more hype. The battle was set between polite, small-town Christians and the aggressive, newcomer Jews. Was Tracey Schager (and her father) some sort of firewall to save rural America? The question was absurd.

Aaron insisted his interest in the city council was about building bridges between the Jews and non-Jews in Postville. The media wanted him to jump into the fray, yell and scream about anti-Semitism, and make the election a mêlée. But from the beginning Aaron insisted the city council seat was not about him, but about Postville. He was, after all, approached by members of the city council to fill an empty seat. Aaron didn't pursue it.

Shortly before the election, Tracey Schager claimed her father began the petition for the special election not because of Aaron himself but because of the way the council handled the appointment. Show-ing signs that the entire affair was wearing her out, Schager told a community forum that if Aaron were voted in, "I think the people of Postville should sup-port him 100 percent."

On April 24, 2001, the special election drew more than 50 percent of eligible voters in Postville. Aaron won handily, by the count of 325 to 216. Only about 3 percent of those votes were cast by Jews. A num-ber of the Jews living in Postville at the time were not American citizens and were therefore ineligible to vote.

Almost all of Aaron's votes came from Christian Postvillians. Clearly, arguments that "the Jews" were taking over Postville were unfounded. The election was a victory for tolerance, decency, and common sense.

On the night of the election, several people gath-ered at Jacob's Table, a kosher restaurant in Postville. When the outcome was announced, Aaron was over-come with emotion and openly wept. The crowd, made up of both of Jews and non-Jews, was exuberant. To her credit, Tracey Schager was conciliatory and gracious. She admitted being surprised by the inten-sity of the media's interest as well as by the anger of Postville residents, including some who accused her of anti-Semitism. Today, Schager and Aaron have a cordial relationship.

Orthodox Jews, many of whom follow the beliefs of Kabbalah (Jewish mysticism) believe that there are no coincidences. Everything happens for some rea-son or another in their view, and it often just takes time for the purpose to reveal itself. Aaron's election became a case in point. When the second edition of Iowa Public Television's Postville documentaries came out, it included an epilogue about Aaron's election with footage from the election-night party. In a voiceover, Aaron explains that Postvillians were more interested in building bridges than exaggerating differences. That voiceover was recorded several months *before* Aaron's appointment to the city council, during the initial filming, and expressed Aaron's hopeful outlook. Yet the words fit the situation perfectly.

Aaron's election was front-page news throughout Iowa and elsewhere. Most newspapers used straightforward headlines such as "Goldsmith Elected to Postville Council," or "Jew Wins Postville Special Election." *The Jewish Press* newspaper used the headline "Victory in Postville."

The satellite trucks left town. The reporters flew home. The media glare trained onto some other communities, and Postville moved on.

Aaron's term ended just six months later. In the meantime, another member of the council died. In November 2001, Aaron ran for his seat without formal opposition, although someone reportedly hatched a write-in campaign at a local bar. Regardless, Aaron won with 99 percent of the vote. This time there were no satellite trucks to be seen. The news was buried in some of the Iowa newspapers, as though it were just another small-town city council election—as the first election was supposed to be. The Associated Press picked up the reelection story, but it didn't launch another full-scale media assault on the community. The city council got on with its work.

Although the media didn't realize it, this second election was more important than the first. This one showed that the ethnicity and religion of the candidate no longer mattered to most Postvillians; they supported Aaron the second time around not because he was an Orthodox Jew but because they believed he was the best person for the job. With his common-sense approach, Aaron could serve as a cultural broker between the diverse groups in town, finding ways to put the community's needs above those of individual ethnicities.

By the time Aaron was elected to the city council, the City of Postville and Agriprocessors had engaged in a number of disputes. One involved annexation of the Agri property. The Rubashkins opposed it, but it passed in a referendum. Then a series of disputes opened up about wastewater treatment facilities and who should pay for expanding these facilities. Agriprocessors depends heavily on them. The dispute was complicated by the use of the city's wastewater lagoons by Iowa Turkey Processors. Aaron was instrumental in negotiations between the city and Agriprocessors; in June 2001, the city and Agri signed an agreement that paved the way for the city to build a new waste treatment facility that met Iowa Department of Natural Resources requirements.

The media glare on Aaron's election in 2001 brought attention from hate groups, white supremacists, and neo-Nazis. These groups started distributing ugly, hate-filled material around town, filled with old, bitterly racist and anti-Semitic stereotypes about Jews and Hispanics. The National Socialist White Revolutionary Party distributed a hideous poem about Latinos. Although some members of the media, particularly those in larger urban states and cities, assumed that this racist material was generated by Iowans and local Postvillians, almost all of them came from organizations outside Iowa.

In addition to the National Socialist White Revolutionary Party, this troubling material came from groups such as the National Alliance and the New Order. The tracts included the usual rhetoric about how Jews "rule" America by controlling the media; claimed that Hitler wasn't such a bad guy after all; insisted that the Holocaust never happened; and noted that Jews had plenty to say about the inferiority of non-Jews. According to the National Alliance, there is a "natural order" of human affairs; the group echoes an apartheid theme through the rhetoric of Hitler, who called for *lebensraum*, or living space, for Aryans. The National Alliance cited the need for "White Living Space." It confidently proclaimed, "We will not be deterred by the difficulty or temporary unpleasantness involved, because we realize that it is absolutely necessary for our racial survival. The long-term demographic trend toward a darker world, which the disastrous policies of the last century have caused, must not only be halted, it must be reversed."

They go on: "We must have new societies throughout the White world that are based on Aryan values and are compatible with the Aryan nature. We do not need to homogenize the White world: there will be room for Germanic societies, Celtics societies, Baltic societies, and so on . . . What we must have, however, is a thorough rooting out of Semitic and other non-Aryan values and customs everywhere . . . this means a society in which young men and women gather to revel with polkas or waltzes, reels or jigs, or any other White dances, but never to undulate or jerk to negroid jazz or rock rhythms. It means pop music without Barry Manilow and art galleries without Marc Chagall." The tracts went on and on with pages of utter racist claptrap. One white supremacist claimed that the influx of minorities and Jews into Iowa was "murdering" the state.

While most of the propaganda was hateful and demeaning, some of it was just bizarre. Postville's mayor, John Hyman, received a signed letter, complete with a return address, containing information from the "CDL," or Christian Defense League (an obvious swipe at the ADL, the Jewish Anti-Defamation League) about the so-called thirteenth tribe of Israel, the Khazars. The letter included a map of Khazaria. The Khazars ruled a powerful empire in central Asia between the seventh and ninth centuries. Many Khazars converted to Judaism. The letter reiterated the old and disproved notion that Ashkenazi, or "European" Jews, are really descendents of the Khazars rather than descendents of Semitic groups in the Middle East: "No one is more anti-Semitic than the Jews who hate their Semitic Arab cousins [who] have more Semitic blood in their veins than Jews." The letter's author offered to send the mayor books from the Christian Patriots Association. The mayor declined.

Reaction to the racist and anti-Semitic propaganda was swift and powerful. Tracey Schager told the press the tracts made her "sick." The mayor, clearly angered and saddened, said an attack on the Jews was an attack on the entire community, and it would not be tolerated. The city council passed a resolution, drafted by Mark, denouncing the propaganda and declaring Postville a community united against hate. With "a resolution embracing the community's ethnic diverse population and protecting citizens by denouncing hate mail literature," the city council resolved "to recognize and embrace the richness and opportunities of ethnically diverse populations; to protect the citizens of Postville by condemning the actions of organizations which distribute materials offensive to residents; and to implore the community to join together and stand up in a united front against racial, cultural, or religious attacks on fellow citizens." Every community and religious leader in town, including several rabbis, lined up to sign the declaration in the glare of TV cameras and other media.

Postville's mayor also sent a letter to the editor of the *Milwaukee Journal Sentinel* responding to propaganda that came from the city's environs.

> *The citizens of Postville and surrounding communities have demonstrated their commitment to making Postville and Northeast Iowa a welcoming and tolerant place for all people regardless of religion, ethnicity, or national origin. The 24 organizations, churches, synagogues, schools and businesses listed below endorsed the April 17, 2001 Postville City Council Resolution Embracing the Community's Ethnically Diverse*

*Populations and Protecting Citizens by Denouncing Hate Mail Literature. In addition, close to 500 citizens from Postville and surrounding communities endorsed this resolution. The good people of Northeast Iowa have recognized that their future is closely tied to building tolerant and respectful communities. They also have shown their desire to live and raise their children in communities that pull together to condemn the forces of hatred and racism.*

It was a brilliant moment. All of Postville rallied.

⊰⊱

Postville came together in other ways, too. One highlight of the town's multicultural outreach efforts was the annual Taste of Postville food festival. Nina Taylor, a local Christian resident, started the festival almost a decade ago as a way of recognizing and celebrating Postville's diversity. In Iowa, as in much of rural America, a town's personality is reflected in its annual community fair. Nina rallied many residents and organized a large, lively celebration. For one weekend each summer, Postville closed three blocks of downtown to traffic, and vendors set up booths to serve foods representing the many cultures in town. There were Israeli falafels, Mexican tacos, Lutheran hot dishes, and much more.

The festival also featured live entertainment, with local and imported acts representing Jews, Latinos, and other cultures in town. At one end of the street, one could watch the traditional Norwegian dancers from a nearby community; at the other end, a Jewish entertainer named Uncle Moishe, flown in from Brooklyn, led the crowd in rousing renditions of Jewish songs in English and Yiddish. The festival was always held on a Sunday so that Sabbath-observing Jews could attend.

The festival was a great success. Hundreds of people from Postville and well beyond attended each year, and everyone mingled, Jews and non-Jews alike. Attendees snatched up T-shirts that read "Postville: A Mosaic in Progress."

As Nina Taylor told the press, the Taste of Postville was designed to "break down the barriers created by a diverse community . . . Once people participate in something, they get to know where their neighbors are coming from, and the barriers begin to break down." The Iowa League of Cities honored the town and the festival with an All-Star Community Award.

Taylor also was instrumental in the development of the Postville Visitor's Center, which was situated in a downtown building and displayed cultural and educational works of the many ethnicities in town. (The visitor's center sold its own T-shirts as well; they read "Postville: The World in One Town.") For a few years before and after the special election, Postville attracted visitors who had heard or read about the town. Busloads of Jews and others arrived to walk the downtown, eat at the kosher restaurant, and shop at the local Latino tiendas. We brought busloads of university faculty, students, church workers, social service providers, teachers, and others to Postville over the years and conducted walking field trips with these groups. Rabbi Schimmel, Nina Taylor, and other champions of diversity were frequent guest lecturers at these events. Visitors particularly enjoyed Taylor's guided tour of the visitor's center.

Radio Postville, a multilingual radio station, was another highlight of the town's efforts to reach out to and embrace its ethnic diversity. The station featured programming in the four major languages of the community. While bilingual radio stations are common in large cities, multilingual stations like Postville's are virtually nonexistent in small-town America.

Radio Postville aired mainly educational programming supplemented by entertainment, comedy, and music. Community health students and staff from the University of Northern Iowa's Global Health Corps regularly recorded disease-prevention and wellness programming in English, Hebrew, Spanish, and Russian; they created more than thirty different radio spots on health issues ranging from breastfeeding to heart disease and tornado safety.

The Postville Soccer League was another beneficiary of Postville's diversity. The league included teams with multiple nationalities and had large audiences of cheering townspeople, as well as local sponsorship. Many of the foreign-born team members grew up playing soccer in their home countries and were a force to be reckoned with in Iowa; Postville's games were unfailingly intense and boisterous.

For many years, Postville's leadership team eagerly received consultations, training, and education from experts on multiculturalism and immigration. Many of these sessions got support from generous external funders such as the Wellmark and Martha Ellen Tye foundations, which aim to help American providers serve minority clients. One especially popular program was an exchange trip to Mexico. In one such trip, former mayor John Hyman, city council member Bob Schroeder, and Nina Taylor experienced firsthand the economic and social conditions that forced many of Postville's newcomers to leave Mexico and migrate to the United States. (On that trip, Bob Schroeder met his future wife, a Mexican woman who now lives in Postville, works for a local social service agency, and serves as a community advocate.)

These achievements in small-town Postville often felt like triumphs of the human spirit, highlighting people's capacity to get along when they have the opportunity to do so. Many of these triumphs came thanks to dedicated locals, diversity champions, and others who worked hard to make Postville shine and showed that multiculturalism can work.

But today, despite these achievements, many ask if diversity has failed in Postville. The town is not what it used to be.

Sadly, many of Postville's efforts to promote tolerance and ethnic understanding have collapsed—at least temporarily—for a variety of reasons, leading people to ask whether Postville is a model for other small towns that struggle with rapid growth in minority and multiethnic populations—or a lesson in what not to do.

Does Postville serve as a blueprint for the nation's future as the baby boomers grow old and minority populations outgrow the white population? When all of our nation's minority populations outnumber the white population, in approximately 2042, will we look back at Postville for guidance, even though its efforts to promote tolerance and understanding have temporarily failed?

Some things that Postville did well—such as creating a bilingual curriculum in the schools—can serve as models for similar communities, but as of 2009, many local residents, former Agri employees, members of the media, and others feel that diversity has died in Postville and the social experiment in multiculturalism has failed.

Part of the problem is that Postville's "small miracles" were not the result of large-scale, well-funded governmental efforts; instead, they were promoted primarily by a small group of impassioned local townspeople and committed external volunteers who were champions of diversity. There was no adequate infrastructure to support change.

Many small towns like Postville—even those that don't face an enormous influx of immigrants and newcomers—suffer from a lack of resources. The federal government has declared many of these rural communities medically underserved areas; they can't provide adequate services for their current residents, let alone for newcomers.

New immigrants, of course, can add to this problem enormously. Towns like Postville suddenly need medical interpreters, cultural liaisons, bilingual teachers, culturally sensitive police, and other services that they never required before.

Providing culturally appropriate services tends to fall to a few highly motivated individuals and non-governmental organizations that champion diversity, multiculturalism, and tolerance. In Postville, such people include Nina Taylor, Merle Turner, Jeff Abbas, Father Paul Oudekirk, Sister Mary McCauley, and Paul Rael from St. Bridget's Catholic Church, Pastor Bracket from St. Paul Lutheran Church and his predecessor, Pastor Bob Hupp, Pastor Catterson from the Presbyterian Church, and a number of other residents from a variety of ethnic groups. When these individuals become overburdened or their organizations become responsible for providing services that government agencies and employers should provide, the system of diversity champions collapses. There are few back-ups to provide support or continue the momentum for the cause. This contributes to the failure of diversity.

This infrastructure has been collapsing in Postville over the past few years. For example, Radio Postville died as a multilingual radio station largely because the local sponsorship and volunteer base was too small. The station tried valiantly to provide programming for major groups in town, but small disagreements over politics got in the way. For example, many Orthodox Jews objected to the station's broadcast of National Public Radio news because they considered it pro-Palestinian. Even the diverse coalition that initially formed the station disbanded. Today, Radio Postville plays mostly American roots music with the occasional talk show (in English); it sometimes broadcasts Hebrew programming. Much of the labor of its tireless, committed producer, Jeff Abbas, goes uncompensated because ongoing financial support is so scarce.

Similarly, when the key players behind the Taste of Postville moved to other towns, the festival ended. And Postville's soccer league ended when the organizer quit and the players were too disorganized or busy to keep it together.

The mayor and city council members who engaged the Jewish and other communities and actively sought to make Postville work—including Aaron and Bob Schroeder—did not seek re-election. Some of the people angriest about the changes in town won seats on the city council, cut funding to the multicultural center, and stopped actively promoting accord among the ethnicities. They hounded those who believed in the new Postville and subjected the former mayor, city clerk, and public works director to a state audit of their financial and other activities.

Working in many rural communities in Iowa and elsewhere, we've seen this syndrome time and again: when key people step down, move away, or otherwise end their involvement, there is no one else to pick up their projects and keep them going. Small, rural communities typically don't have the critical mass of trained, passionate replacements to cover for key community organizers who might leave. That's one lesson from Postville, but it just scratches the surface of what went wrong.

There are other, far more complicated reasons that Postville's experiment in diversity failed— temporarily or otherwise. Ultimately, these broader reasons don't have much to do with the heroic activism of those who want to make a multicultural town work or those who believe in diversity for diversity's sake. Their good efforts were apparent and praiseworthy, but lurking underneath them, and the whole town, were the powerful forces of a new world economic order and the age-old temptation to exploit vulnerable populations that ultimately made it impossible for the new Postville to become a true community.

These other forces at work in Postville overcame much of the goodwill of dozens of caring local individuals from myriad backgrounds. Unfortunately, these same forces may overcome the best intentions in similar small towns as well, and perhaps affect wide swaths of our society in the future as rural America undergoes demographic change and globalization.

# CHAPTER FOUR

# The Fall of the Empire

THE NATIONAL CATTLE CONGRESS in Waterloo, Iowa, is like a county fairground on steroids. It's anchored by the aging McElroy Auditorium, one of those classic venues where so much beer has spilled that no amount of cleaning can keep your shoes from sticking to the floor. The local minor-league hockey team played there for decades until a new arena was built in downtown Waterloo in the 1990s. The auditorium still hosts rodeos, country music concerts, and cage fights on occasion.

Several big, warehouse-like buildings called pavilions surround the Cattle Congress and are used to host events such as gun shows. One of the pavilions was converted into a party hall some years ago and is rented out for community celebrations, weddings, and the like. The grounds also contain a classic dance hall called the Electric Park Ballroom. It harkens back to the days of the big bands and early rockers such as Buddy Holly.

The rest of the buildings are designed to house livestock. They are long, brick structures built decades ago, when the Cattle Congress was known as the National Dairy Cattle Congress and farmers and dairy industry officials came from across North America. Those glory days, when the Cattle Congress competed with the famous Iowa State Fair, are long gone. Today the facility has a surreal look and the haunting feel of a bygone era, when the family farm was alive and well and people met *en masse* to celebrate their rural heritage. Nowadays, the Cattle Congress hosts only small events, with limited attendance. (Still, children like Michele's son Daniel display avid competitive streaks when they show their chickens and goats during the 4-H summer fair. They're hoping to be selected for the Iowa State Fair in August.)

In the spring of 2008, thousands of Jews, Christians, local Postvillians, Mexicans, Guatemalans, Salvadorans, Russians, and others far beyond northeast Iowa had no warning that their lives would soon be abruptly and irreparably changed by an event that began in the Cattle Congress. The tired Cattle Congress fairgrounds unexpectedly sprang to life again. The grounds began to swarm with small armies of contractors, trucks, and construction machinery. Although most of the work took place in the buildings and out of sight from the street, it was obvious something big was happening. Rumors really started swirling when contractors attached massive ventilation tubing systems to some of the pavilions.

Word spread that the Federal Emergency Management Agency (FEMA) was in town and was responsible for what was happening at the Cattle

Congress. But why? The rumors kept piling up. Word leaked that FEMA was installing chain-link fences and bunk beds inside the buildings. The manager of the Cattle Congress, who leased the property to FEMA, claimed he didn't know what the organization was up to. But it appeared that FEMA was preparing to hold a massive number of people in the Cattle Congress buildings.

Some speculated that FEMA was performing a drill in preparation for the next Hurricane Katrina (although they couldn't explain why such a drill would require chain-link holding facilities). Other stories, often unleashed in local hotel bars by federal agents disguising themselves as officials from the United States Department of Agriculture, suggested the buildings were being prepared for a drill in case of an agro-terrorism event. Fringe groups, which always suspect the federal government is about to declare martial law and take away citizens' guns and other freedoms, got into the act. Their websites were full of photos from the Cattle Congress and speculation that FEMA, which they believe will lead the charge to deny citizen rights, was preparing a detention facility for those who failed to fall into line with the new order of affairs. Roguegovernment.com reported, "Plans for government run concentration camps are well documented . . . . This looks like a continuation of this concentration camp agenda and considering that the government has refused to take real action to stop the illegal alien problem, why would they want to build a FEMA camp in the middle of

Iowa to run a drill? The answer is simple. They are going to use the excuse of the illegal alien problem to setup the FEMA camp infrastructure which will be used to house the average Americans who protest what this corrupt and out of control government has been doing."

Local officials in the Waterloo area wanted to know what was going on at the Cattle Congress, too. Tom O'Rourke, the longtime, ever-vigilant director of the Black Hawk County Health Department, demanded to know if the Cattle Congress was being prepared for a terrorism or natural disaster drill; federal agencies gave him, at best, misleading or incomplete information. County Emergency Medical Services (EMS) personnel were not informed, either, as they would have been if FEMA were preparing for a natural-disaster drill. Even most law-enforcement agents were kept in the dark until the very end.

But people in the immigration business suspected what was about to happen: the Immigration and Customs Enforcement (ICE) agency of the federal government was preparing for a big raid. All the signs were there. In addition to the many contractors and construction workers at the site, there were increasing numbers of people dressed in hunting jackets and camouflage hats. They obviously weren't construction workers. Some of them stood at the front gate, stopping cars and asking for IDs, yet they wore no uniforms and had no visible firearms.

We drove to the front gate once and said, "We just want to know what is going on." The man we

spoke to didn't want to talk to us. When we reminded him that the Cattle Congress was a public facility
and said we just wanted to "look around," he became
very official and uptight, refusing to identify himself
and demanding identification from us. We drove
away. (The next week, after the raid, we saw the same
man at the Cattle Congress wearing an official ICE
agent jacket.)

As the weeks wore on, the local hotels and mo-
tels filled up. Hotels in Cedar Rapids and other
towns within a two-hour drive started to fill as well.
ICE officials told the media they couldn't discuss the
operation and provided no specific information. Rumors that ICE, or *la migra* in Mexican slang, was in
town spread like wildfire among Latinos and their
advocates.

Immigration attorneys and other advocates organized an information session after the Spanish-
language mass at the Queen of Peace Church in
Waterloo. A similar informational session was
planned for Postville, but it came too late.

We were certain that a raid was going to take
place soon, but were unsure where. The likely candidate was a meatpacking plant, but which one? ICE
had raided the Swift packing plant in nearby Mar-
shalltown in December 2006 and probably wouldn't
raid it again so soon. The large pork plant in Waterloo was another candidate, but the company that
owns the plant, Tyson, seemed to have its political
ducks in a row with ICE. The logical candidate was
Agriprocessors in Postville. The plant was overdue

for a raid, frankly, given the rampant rumors about how many people worked there without proper immigration documents.

On May 12, 2008, the day after the information session at the Waterloo Queen of Peace Church, ICE swept into Postville and the Agri plant. Apparently, plant officials knew that ICE was going to move in but they were told the action would take place on May 13. ICE surprised them and arrived a day earlier. The raid started promptly at 10 a.m.

In some ways, it was a classic immigration raid, with two helicopters flying overhead, dozens of federal and state law enforcement officials from ICE, federal marshals, the Iowa State Patrol, and multiple ICE buses lined up to haul away their human cargo.

But ICE had learned some things from criticism of their previous raids, and they changed many of their tactics in the Postville raid. For example, instead of gathering all of the employees *en masse* and then questioning everyone about their citizenship or immigration status, they divided the employees into groups: those who could verify their immigration status, and those who could not.

Of course, the overwhelming number of employees fell into the latter category. ICE checked their names in computer databases. Within three hours, 398 people were detained, packed into ICE buses and driven to the Cattle Congress in Waterloo. At the time, it was the largest single site raid of a U.S. employer. We found out later that ICE entered Postville and the Agri premises with arrest warrants for nearly 700 workers, which remains a national record for an immigration raid.

ICE did its best to deceive the press and others about the location and timing of the raid. It sent decoy convoys from the Cattle Congress to throw the press off the trail. One of our contacts in the media followed one of these decoys and ended up at a truck stop about ten miles from the Cattle Congress. The ICE team pulled in, bought themselves some coffee, and stood around in the parking lot chatting while the raid was taking place in Postville, some eighty miles away.

Thanks to contacts, inside information, or pure luck, many members of the media were at the Agri site when the raid started. More arrived shortly afterward. For several days, Postville was inundated with media from around the world, just as it had been during Aaron's special election. The media was also well represented at the Cattle Congress. They were there when the ICE buses arrived and for weeks after.

≫·≪

ICE ended its charade of preparing for an agroterrorism drill, and the Cattle Congress became a fully staffed and functioning temporary field prison. Federal agents stopped wearing their contractor cloths and donned their ICE or Federal Marshal jackets and carried their side arms. Non-law enforcement personnel, such as Department of Homeland Security (DHS) attorneys, moved from trailer to trailer on the main parking lot. The front gate became a check-point; only official vehicles were allowed to pass, and other visitors were searched and vetted. Those with official business, such as public defenders and immigration attorneys, had to surrender their driver's licenses upon entering.

Even those with the appropriate badges were allowed to move on the grounds only if accompanied by an armed escort. ICE wouldn't allow the detainees' families and the media to stand at the chain link fence surrounding the Cattle Congress; they were forced to observe the proceedings from a sidewalk across the street. Security personnel at the facility were strict but generally cordial, and many even used humor. It was obvious they'd been trained to be polite.

The day after the raid, we were invited to join a group of immigration attorneys who visited the Cattle Congress grounds. These attorneys arrived from throughout Iowa to provide their services *pro bono*. They asked us to help them with some language and cultural interpretation issues, knowing that we work with detainees from several cultures, including Israelis.

Security guards held us at the front gate for more than an hour while confirming that we sure should be allowed in. After being searched and turning in our driver's licenses, we got visitor IDs and were escorted to a FEMA trailer. After entering the trailer, we were allowed to leave it for only two reasons: to use the restroom or to leave the grounds. ICE even forbade the use of cell phones.

In the end, we spent about seven hours with the attorneys in the FEMA trailer. We weren't allowed to get food where the ICE people ate, so the lawyers ordered pizza. The poor teenager who delivered the pizzas to the front gate was himself an immigrant from Bosnia; he found himself surrounded and questioned by overtly polite federal marshals, who examined the pizza before we were allowed to eat it.

The immigration attorneys had filed the required paperwork naming specific detainees who had the right to legal counsel. But the feds still weren't going to allow the attorneys to see any detainees in the facility. DHS attorneys visited the detainees a few times and knew the workers had the right to see their immigration attorneys. Still, DHS had no intention of letting them do so, because it was considering felony criminal charges against them—not less-serious administrative immigration violations. We knew the fix was in when, at about 3:00 p.m., federal public defenders and a federal court judge from Cedar Rapids appeared outside the FEMA trailer.

We finally left the Congress grounds at about 4 p.m. We were frustrated but none the worse for wear. Over the next few days, some of the immigration attorneys were allowed to see a handful of clients, but even these visits were limited.

We later learned just how deeply the fix was in for the Postville detainees, thanks to one of the court interpreters. Dr. Erik Camayd-Freixas was one of twenty-six federal court-certified Spanish interpreters flown to Waterloo to process detainees through the makeshift courts on the Cattle Congress grounds.

Camayd is a professor at Florida International University, where he runs one of the nation's top interpreter and translator training programs. Camayd has been a federally certified court interpreter for twenty-three years. In all that time, he never publicly questioned whether the court proceedings he was interpreting violated his clients' rights. (In general, it is very rare for federal court interpreters to criticize court procedures or personnel, including judges.) But after his first day working in the Waterloo ICE detention center and courts and experiencing firsthand the abuses and systematic disregard for the detainees' civil and human rights, he spoke out.

Camayd wrote a disturbing essay on June 13, 2008, entitled "Interpreting after the Largest ICE Raid in U.S. History: A Personal Account." His intended audience was his fellow interpreters, but the essay was leaked to hundreds of others in the immigration and legal professions. It caught the attention of Julia Preston, an immigration reporter at the *New York Times*, who then wrote a front-page article about it. A few weeks later, Camayd found himself testifying before Congress.

We met Camayd twice: once in Minnesota and once in Postville. Camayd is an affable, knowledgeable, and dignified man, a Cuban immigrant who descends from Maronite Christians in Lebanon. His interpretation skills are so widely respected that he provided the interpreted voice on Spanish-language television networks of several U.S. presidential candidates during their campaigns and debates. He joked,

"I have been Barack Obama three times!" It was easy for us to see why the situation at the Cattle Congress affected him so deeply.

Camayd described his three principal concerns about the Postville detainees' treatment. First, most of the detainees were indigenous people from Guatemala who were functionally illiterate, and Spanish was not their first language. Most were unaware that they needed Social Security numbers to work in the U.S. They didn't know what a Social Security number *was*. They assumed—reasonably enough—that they were in court because they had entered the United States illegally. But they soon found out they were facing very different charges—felony criminal charges.

Secondly, Camayd was appalled by the lack of due process afforded the detainees. Defendants were marched ten at a time through meetings with their attorneys and hearings; attorneys had very little time to talk to their clients or investigate their cases. Camayd described the process as the "saddest procession I have ever witnessed . . . . Driven single-file in groups of ten, shackled at the wrists, waist and ankles, chains dragging as they shuffled through, the slaughterhouse workers were brought in for arraignment, sat and listened through headsets to the interpreted initial appearance, before marching out again." As one of his interpreter colleagues commented, "When I saw what it was really about, my heart sank."

The third problem with the Cattle Congress courts had to do with why we and the immigration attorneys didn't get access to clients. Namely, ICE attorneys never intended to charge the detainees with immigration violations.

The Postville raid was unique because of the way ICE and the federal court worked together before the event to set up the detainees. In the majority of immigration raids prior to Postville, detainees were generally charged with administrative immigration violations and deported. But in the Postville case, the majority of detainees were forced into a plea bargain agreement in which their choices were to accept one of two felony convictions. The detainees were given a choice: they could plead guilty to one set of felony charges and receive five months in jail and deportation, or they could face the prospect of much more serious charges and a considerably longer jail term.

Here is how Camayd explained it in his essay: "By handing down the inflated charge of 'aggravated identity theft,' which carries a mandatory minimum sentence of two years in prison, the government forced the defendants into pleading guilty to the lesser charge and accepting five months in jail. Clearly, without the inflated charge, the government had no bargaining leverage, because the lesser charge by itself, using a false Social Security number, carries only a discretionary sentence of zero to six months. The judges would be free to impose sentence within those guidelines, depending on the circumstances of each case and any prior record. Virtually all the defendants would have received only probation and been immediately deported. In fact, the government's offer at the higher end of the guidelines (one month shy of the maximum sentence) was indeed no bargain. What is worse, the inflated charge, via the binding 11(C)(1)(c) Plea Agreement, reduced the judges to mere bureaucrats, pronouncing the same litany over and over for the record in order to legalize the proceedings, but having absolutely no discretion or decision-making power. As a citizen, I want our judges to administer justice, not a federal agency."

These sentiments were echoed at a meeting two months later, on September 18, 2008. We were stuck all day in the back row of a Kansas City hotel ballroom filled with about 200 attorneys, mostly immigration attorneys and federal public defenders who had flown in from around the country. The meeting's title was "Post-Postville Criminal Defense Training," but it was really a postmortem. The purpose was to learn about and discuss attorneys' experiences during and after the raid, lessons from the experience, and ways public defenders and other attorneys for immigrants could prepare themselves for the next immigration raid.

The first presenters were full-time federal public defenders and court-appointed public defenders who played roles in the aftermath of the Postville raid. Two of the public defenders explained the impossible situation in which they found themselves during and after the raid. On May 12, the lead federal court judge in Cedar Rapids summoned them to a meeting; they were forbidden to discuss the matter with their bosses. They, along with some of the court-appointed defenders, arrived at the appointed time, 10:30. They were informed that ICE had commenced a full-scale raid on the Postville plant thirty minutes earlier, and that they were expected to go to Waterloo and defend the detainees in federal court proceedings. At least one of the court-appointed defenders refused to play along, citing ethical concerns.

Until they got to the Cattle Congress grounds the next day, the defenders didn't realize that they would be defending detainees ten at a time, or that they wouldn't have time to interview the detainees or conduct any kind of research on their behalf. The attorneys were handed a script, or manual, prepared months ahead of time by the court with help from U.S. attorneys, outlining the charges that would be brought against their clients, the plea bargains that would be made available to them, and the judges' plans for processing the detainees.

The federal public defenders were in an impossible situation. How were they to adequately defend ten clients at a time, in the face of a forced, predetermined plea bargain? The defenders might have refused to cooperate with the court on ethical grounds, and many at the Kansas City attorneys' conference suggested that they should have done so. In the halls and elevators outside the conference, some attorneys stated openly that the Cedar Rapids defenders should be disbarred for practicing under such unethical conditions and for failing to act in the best interests of their clients. Others noted that the public defenders did the best they could, without the luxury of time or reflection.

Those attorneys who aimed their anger at their Iowa colleagues should instead have trained it on the court. Not only did the court apparently know in advance about the Postville raid, but it also prepared for the legal proceedings afterward. As far as we can tell, this was unprecedented. Many critics noted that the court, rather than being an impartial deliberator, decided well in advance that the detainees were guilty and wouldn't be allowed to seek justice through any semblance of a fair trial.

Attorney Peter Moyers served as a clerk in the Northern District of Iowa during the raid and the Cattle Congress proceedings. He wrote his own analysis of the situation, based on interviews with a handful of defense attorneys, his review of the case law, and media accounts. He claimed the script, or manual, the court developed wasn't the problem and didn't lead to coercion. Nor was a lack of knowledge among defendants the problem. Rather, he claimed, "the coercion involved flowed from the law itself . . . . The defendants understood their limited choices all too well: put the government to its proof and exercise one's rights, and risk at least two years imprisonment, or take the deal and spend no more than five months out of work." The attorneys Moyers interviewed "emphasized the importance of certainty for their clients, who were anxious about when they could return to their families . . . the prospect of a minimum two-year prison term made the offer of five months exceedingly attractive."

Yet the question remained: Why were the Agri workers forced into the plea bargain in the first place? Why were the Agri workers criminalized when previous immigrant actions placed the emphasis on deportation? One defense attorney Moyers interviewed told a client that the U.S. Attorney's Office "hoped that upon their return to their countries of origin, [they] would tell their stories and thereby discourage others from seeking unlawful entry and employment in the Northern District of Iowa."

Criticism of the Postville detainees' treatment was widespread and angry. While strictly within the law, the forced plea bargains raised concerns about human rights; it also led many to ask whether the real issue at a stake was illegal immigration, not illegal employment. Two months after the Postville raid, ICE conducted another, even larger immigration raid in Mississippi. The federal court judge responsible for overseeing the proceedings didn't know about the raid until the day it happened; as soon as he found out, he informed the local public defenders. The vast majority of the Mississippi detainees were charged with administrative immigration charges and deported, as had been the standard practice for several years. A handful were charged with felony identify theft or unlawful use of a Social Security number.

Was the lack of prior court involvement in Mississippi, or the fact that most detainees received the traditional immigration violation charges a response to criticism of how the Postville situation was handled? It's impossible to say.

The federal court's involvement in preparing for the Postville raid and its aftermath may have been unique, because the head court judge was willing to collaborate with the U.S. Attorney. When one of the Latino managers at Agriprocessors was later arrested and brought to court in Cedar Rapids, his attorneys requested that the judge hearing his case recuse herself because of her bias, as demonstrated in her cooperation with prosecutors in the Postville raid. She refused.

Another case in point: Michele went to the Cattle Congress on the third day after the raid. Because Michele speaks Hebrew and is known by a number of the Jews in Postville, the families of two Israeli detainees asked her to go the facility and inquire about their well-being. They wanted to make sure the detainees were getting kosher food (they were) and find out if and when they would be released (one would be, but the other remained in custody.) Michele drove to the facility and parked in the small lot next to the guard shack, where the attorneys and consular delegations parked. She talked to several agents and security personnel about the status of the Israelis. She didn't get much information, and she was not allowed to see the detainees.

However, DHS personnel became suspicious of Michele. Investigators were exploring the possibility that one of the Israeli detainees had married an American citizen to obtain a green card, and then later divorced her and married an Israeli woman without satisfying the terms of his initial visa. In short, he was potentially facing charges of immigration fraud. Michele's familiarity with his situation in Postville and her fluency in Hebrew set off alarms for DHS officials.

While Michele chatted with security personnel near her car, three DHS vehicles and half a dozen agents surrounded her and her son, who had come along for the ride. They questioned Michele for more than twenty minutes before she satisfied them that she was not the detainee's alleged American wife. After the matter was cleared up, she finally was allowed to leave the Cattle Congress grounds.

→←

The Cattle Congress was equipped to hold as many as 700 detainees. The ICE issued 700 arrest warrants: only 389 detainees were held. After the *Des Moines Register* filed a Freedom of Information suit, the ICE issued a press release stating that had spent $5.2 million of taxpayer funds on the raid. This estimate does not include other costs, such as the Federal Court for the Northern District of Iowa's expenditures on interpreters, travel, felony trials, public defenders, detainee imprisonment, and deportation fees. The *Des Moines Register* cited detainee prison costs of nearly $600,000 a month by mid-summer, and noted that it was already costing taxpayers an average of $13,396 for each of the 389 illegal immigrants taken into custody.

For weeks, an eerie glow from the Congress grounds dominated the Waterloo sky at night and was visible from twenty miles away. This aura came from the dozens of high-powered lights set up around the grounds. It was strange enough to see fairgrounds outfitted with holding cells, FEMA trailers, and massive ventilation tubes attached to the pavilions where we had attended events many times. But at night, the bright lights gave the place the feel of a concentration camp. Some of our colleagues referred to the site as the Guantanamo Bay of Iowa.

Outside, a sizeable group of concerned citizens and protestors marched to protest the raid and U.S. immigration policy. They held candlelight vigils several nights in a row, in a parking lot across the street from the guard shack. Many members of the media were present as well. The DHS guards and ICE agents were generally careful to be polite and proper with detainees, visitors, and protestors alike, but were nonetheless unmoved by the large gathering across the street from the Cattle Congress. They knew that all the lighted candles in the world at that time would not make a difference. The fate of the detainees was already sealed, and most would ultimately be imprisoned and deported.

# CHAPTER FIVE

# Sent Reeling:
# Postville After the Raid

THE RAID HAD A DEVASTATING IMPACT on Postville in the weeks and months immediately following the event. Nearly 400 people were arrested initially during the raid, primarily line and plant workers who were low-level migrant laborers. Weeks later, Shalom Rubashkin and key members of his Agriprocessors management team were also arrested on dozens of charges of harboring illegal aliens, money laundering, violating safety regulations, and other serious crimes under state and federal law, including an astonishing 9,300 charges of individual daily violations of child labor laws. Eventually, about half of the plant's workforce was arrested. True to Postville's multicultural nature, the arrestees and those charged included an array of ethnicities, including American Jews, local white Christians, Israelis, Guatemalans, Ukrainians, Mexicans, and even an Arab.

The overwhelming majority of the migrant laborers arrested right after the raid were Guatemalan peasants, many of Mayan Indian descent, who were poor laborers or highland villagers back home with low education and literacy levels. They were sent to the detention center in Waterloo. Women who took care of young children got ICE geographic positioning system (GPS) tracking devices and were allowed to stay—but not work—in Postville. Other immigrants who escaped the raid—or were just afraid—sought sanctuary in St. Bridget's Catholic Church. As the parish sister noted during a press conference, it was a human tragedy.

We have witnessed poverty and the crowded chaos of refugee camps in many parts of the world, but the scene in the Postville church was one of the most astonishing things we have ever seen. It reminded us we don't need to travel to foreign lands to witness mass displacement of human beings.

Some 350 Latinos—adults and children—were jammed into the church, sleeping on and under pews and taking their meals in the fellowship hall. Local churches and civic organizations stepped up to provide meals, clothing, and other necessities. The school bus diverged from its usual route to pick up and deliver children to the church. The church provided spiritual sanctuary; some of the Guatemalans, confused and desperate, also hoped it could provide legal sanctuary. Many stayed at the church for several days, until they were reasonably sure they weren't going to be apprehended by *la migra*.

Formerly optimistic townspeople could find had no encouraging words; they could express only anger and disgust. The situation had no silver lining. Overnight, Postville became a kind of post-immigrant town, or at least a post-Latino town. ICE had arrested about 20 percent of the town's entire population; many more fled or went into hiding.

After the raid, rabbis who worked at Agriprocessors scrambled to process some of the remaining meat products to keep them from rotting. But for all intents and purposes, the plant shut down for about three weeks. In an effort to get it up and running again, Agri hired staffing agencies to recruit and hire new workers. But they had a challenge: attracting people to work in a small, isolated town, in a meat plant that had undergone a massive immigration raid and faced charges of employee abuse—all for low wages.

The solution was to find people who were desperate for work. Agri hired several external staffing agencies to help recruit all kinds of people from all over who could legally work in the United States and replace those employees who had been working illegally in the plant: homeless people from Texas, African Americans from Ohio and Tennessee, Native Americans from Nebraska, Palauans from the Pacific, and secondary migrants from large Midwestern cities who originally came from Somalia and other African nations.

Most of these recruits didn't work in the plant very long—in some cases, they lasted just a few days. Some were fired; many others quit because the job was difficult and distasteful. In many cases, the recruiters didn't come through with their generous promises of fair wages, housing assistance, and benefits, and workers found themselves stranded in the community without sufficient resources.

People flowed into and out of Postville so quickly that the town seemed to change on a daily basis. Recruiters hired ex-convicts and people just out of rehab centers, giving the town an uneasy edge. Crime rates increased

One particularly troubling incident involved a newcomer who had worked hard in the plant but didn't get paid. After leaving the town in anger, he gave an interview to Radio Postville about his experience. The station never aired the interview, but a Minnesota website released it, and Postville law enforcement officials heard it. During the interview, the man—who was never named—said disgruntled workers from the plant planned to commit robberies and even kidnappings in Postville because "they didn't get the money they worked for." He also reported conversations about kidnapping the family members of Shalom Rubashkin because they heard he had lots of money in his house. The Postville police took the claims seriously and increased patrols near Jewish facilities. Some townspeople were concerned. Others felt that sharing the information was unnecessary sensationalism. In the end, the threatened robberies and kidnappings never happened.

Despite the efforts of Agri's recruiting agencies, the plant couldn't find or keep enough legal workers to get back up to its pre-raid production levels. Slaughtering and processing animals and turning them into meat products requires hundreds of individual steps. Each step involves at least one worker; some steps require dozens. A meat plant can't function with a skeleton crew.

The Agri plant didn't just slaughter animals and produce meat products like steaks; it also made processed products such as kosher hotdogs and lunch meats. A lot of value is added to the animal after the prime cuts are removed. Plants can't produce, package, store, and ship these more profitable products without an adequate workforce.

Because Agri couldn't find and retain enough legal workers, the plant barely managed to operate one shift of its poultry line. This remained the case a year after the raid. The beef line never reopened.

Many new plant employees had difficulties with the firms that recruited them. One firm paid people with debit cards, a practice that was unfamiliar to the majority of foreign-born workers. Employees received a pay slip showing their hours, amount earned, et cetera, but their pay was deposited in a bank account in South Dakota. Workers had to use their debit cards to draw from the account locally. The practice is legal if workers sign a consent form, but since many of the new hires couldn't read English, it's unlikely they knew what they were signing.

Some of these workers shared their experience with us. Postville had only a couple of ATMs where they could get cash. The ATMs had withdrawal limits, so employees who wanted to withdraw large amounts for a purchase, or who wanted to withdraw all their funds and leave town, were out of luck. The local grocery store accepted the ATM cards for groceries, but wouldn't give cash back. Other businesses didn't take the cards at all.

Workers were also troubled by automatic pay deductions, including "conveyance" charges and other fees. A local housing company automatically deducted workers' rent. It justified this action, because it noted that many of the workers were transient and unreliable in paying their rents. Worker advocates countered that rates of up to $200 per person per mattress per month in crowded, poorly maintained houses were outrageous and exploitive. In the end, most temporary workers ended up with very little or no net income. Their pay slips accumulated in advocates' offices until finally the media exposed the problem.

Despite such problems, immigrants and refugees arrived in growing numbers. At one point, there were about 100 Somali and other African refugees in Postville. Most came from St. Paul, Minnesota, looking for work and a quiet, safe community. Some came from neighborhoods with growing crime rates, and they appreciated the relative calm of Postville. An Ethiopian man who recruited many of Agriprocessor's Africans workers opened a small store and called it Peace Grocery in honor of the town, where—for at least a brief period—people from five nations of his native continent lived together in harmony.

The Somalis opened a makeshift mosque and a small tea shop where men gathered to play dominos and gossip. They covered the mosque's windows with rugs for privacy. For a few weeks, several dozen people worshipped there daily. The Somali Muslim women wore traditional clothing, including *hijab* to cover the sides of their faces and hair. They made a striking image when they walked down the street in their flowing, colorful gowns. Some wore their head scarves so tightly they could stick their opened cell phones between their *hijab* and their ear and they could talk on the phone with their hands free—a homemade Bluetooth.

But the Africans workers didn't stay for long. Like many other plant employees, they grew disgruntled over wages, debit card payments, and the work itself. Some were also unhappy that they weren't allowed to pray at the plant. By January 2009, only a handful of African workers remained. The mosque, tea shop, and Peace Grocery shut down.

In fall 2008, dozens of workers and their families arrived from the tiny nation of Palau, in the North Pacific. The Palauan ambassador to the U.S. had visited Postville earlier that year; after meeting with the mayor and Agri officials, he approved the recruitment of his countrymen. The Palauans were attractive recruits; as residents of a former protectorate of the United States, they were legally eligible to work in Postville; they spoke English; and they came from an island nation with high unemployment, so they weren't likely to hurry back.

But like most other populations that arrived after the raid, the Palauans didn't last long. Many felt they were recruited under false pretenses. Facing problems with expensive housing and wages, they demanded that their ambassador come to Postville to assist them.

In another remarkable Postville moment, dozens of angry Palauans gathered in the town's multicultural center to confront their hapless ambassador. In the end, nothing came of their protests, and in subsequent weeks the majority of Palauans scattered. Before they left, many Postville residents gave them warm clothing to replace their colorful shorts and sandals so they could survive the frigid Iowa winter.

The demise of Postville's largest employer brought the town and region to its economic knees. The plant's closure was the first in a series of falling dominos. After it fell, the local cattle producers were next in line. Agriprocessors hadn't paid the producers in some time, and when the plant closed, the producers lost the only major cattle buyer for hundreds of miles. They were forced to look elsewhere to sell their livestock.

Then there were the thousands of chickens, most owned by a subsidiary of Agriprocessors, that were ready or near-ready for slaughter when Agriprocessors shut down. Many feared that thousands of chickens would be left to die of starvation and dehydration before they ever made it to the kill line, since Agri no longer had credit with the feed providers. But the bank holding most of Agri's debt released enough money to pay the feed bill, keep the chickens alive, and reopen the plant, just in time to process the chickens that were ready for slaughter.

Meanwhile, Postville's economic situation quickly deteriorated. Within days of the raid, El Vaquero, a large clothing store serving the Mexican community, closed its doors. The Guatemalan food store was forced to give up its lease and merge with a small restaurant; it began selling a fraction of the food and other products it had offered before. The other large tienda and restaurant in town, the popular Sabor Latino, lost many of its customers in the months after the raid and was forced to downsize. Desperate for cash, the owners installed pool and foosball tables, hoping to bring in people to play games for a buck or two.

The kosher store fell on hard times too. After losing jobs at the plant, Jewish workers and their families had less money to spend at the store. Without sufficient funds to buy supplies, the store began rationing staples such as milk. Many of the store's financial assets were mired in money-laundering charges against Agri's owner, Shalom Rubashkin, and suppliers were unwilling to provide food to a store with no credit that was mired in a criminal scandal related to the raid. Customers started telephone networks to alert each other when kosher dairy products and other coveted items arrived at the store. Jewish communities on the East Coast and elsewhere—including the Sons of Jacob Synagogue in Waterloo, Iowa, and a committed large Jewish Community Action relief effort from the Twin Cities—donated kosher supplies to help the store survive.

The plant closing also had a serious impact on local housing. There are two large housing companies in Postville. One is Nevel Properties, a subsidiary of Agri owned in part by the Rubashkin family. The other is GAL investments, owned by an Israeli Jew who came to Postville several years earlier. Both Nevel and GAL housed plant workers after the plant shut down. Both deducted high rents and fees directly from the workers' paychecks. In general, this arrangement worked as long as workers kept their jobs. But then the plant closed, and the housing domino fell.

Recruiting companies stopped collecting rent from plant workers, because the workers were no longer collecting paychecks. Angry workers, unable to pay their rent, simply left town; some committed minor acts of vandalism, such as leaving water running to overflow sinks and ruin floors. Others were evicted when they couldn't make their monthly rent payments. Many people stopped paying for utilities, and shutoffs mounted. Applications for state heating assistance piled up.

More and more workers left town, leaving many rental units empty. No renters meant no rent, and no income for the housing companies to pay their bills to local suppliers and service providers. With fewer residents, the city's revenue from water and sewage hookups dropped like a rock. Providing these services to the rest of community left the town in debt.

With a rapidly declining economy, a churning and unstable population, and growing homelessness came a ballooning demand for basic services, including food. In desperation, townspeople established an emergency food and crisis center in the multicultural center that houses Radio Postville. The station manager, Jeff Abbas, and dozens of residents worked around the clock for days to provide hot meals, clothes, and emotional support to displaced workers. Others in town, particularly risk-averse community center board members and overwhelmed local politicians, criticized the crisis center, which operated during a period when the mayor was on an extended elk-hunting vacation in Colorado.

Upon his return, and in recognition of the significant local and national negative attention that was accumulating about Postville, Mayor Penrod asked Iowa governor Chet Culver to declare Postville a "human and economic disaster area." The state didn't formally grant this request. However, several weeks later—and six months after the raid—Iowa's Lieutenant Governor, Patty Judge, visited Postville. She offered the services of three Americorps volunteers to assist with relief efforts and promised funding for rental assistance.

Postville was in dire straits for months after the raid. Many locals volunteered their time, labor, and money to help the Latinos sheltered by the Catholic church and elsewhere. The generous outpouring of sympathy and support for these people lasted for several months. However, because these Guatemalan detainees couldn't work or leave the area, they were particularly dependent on cash donations and the local food bank, both of which benefited from Christian church groups in the area. More than 150 people lined up weekly at the local food bank several times a week, including Latinos, whites, Palauans, African Americans, Somalis, and others struggling to survive in post-raid Postville.

The stress proved too much for many in town, and the social and economic burden of care for displaced workers grew enormous. Tensions ran high among different cultural groups that had worked closely together for years. Overworked volunteer staff at the local Catholic church felt that they bore the heaviest burden of caring for the Guatemalan detainees, while others cited their own organizational efforts to feed the hungry and meet the needs of other ethnic populations in the community.

Most townspeople were united, though, in their feelings that the plant owners should have contributed more to the relief efforts for displaced workers after the raid. They expected the plant to provide regular, large donations of food to displaced workers, and to at least offer ongoing emotional support, reassurance, and referrals to those laid off or arrested, if they could not pay them outright. Agri officials countered that plant managers visited the Catholic church right after the raid to tell Latino workers where they could pick up their final paychecks, and said the plant sometimes donated meat to the food bank. They noted that most of the rabbis in town were unavailable to help with relief efforts because they were working night and day in the plant—without pay—trying to keep the business running and save products from spoiling.

In addition to the economic crisis, Postville became the epicenter of an ongoing national debate about immigration reform. To us, the situation became a glaring human disaster. In newspaper articles, editorials, and radio broadcasts, we encouraged people to think about the human implications of a broken immigration system. As we stated in one opinion piece, "As long as we have an immigration system that provides incentives for the undocumented to risk working here illegally and provides incentives for employers to exploit these desperate workers, situations like that in Postville will continue. [Our nation has] set up a system that rewards immigrants and employers to cheat, and then we unfairly blame the workers and their families for being here in the first place."

A few months after the raid, two Agri supervisors and two members of the human resources department pleaded guilty to federal immigration violations, including harboring illegal immigrants. These guilty pleas brought a return of the intense glare of international media to Postville, and the town was inundated with journalists asking questions about immigration reform. Mayor Bob Penrod told CNN the ICE raid turned Postville "topsy turvy . . . . It makes a person feel kind of angry. It's been nothing but a freaky nightmare since May." Aaron told the network, "They took a problem that needed a 22-caliber bullet, and they dropped a nuclear bomb on us. They made a poster child out of us. They turned people into cattle. If ICE really wanted to address the immigration problem, it should have gone to some place like Los Angeles; it didn't because "there's too much political clout. So they go to a place where there's no political backbone. They go to a place where the government's willing to throw us to the dogs." The ICE raid in Postville also ignited a firestorm of controversy among Jews about the role of labor in kosher food production, which we will discuss in a subsequent chapter.

⇒⇐

The debates about immigration and, by extension, diversity, soon took center stage in the media after the Postville raid. In many cases, these debates forced people into artificial camps and into forms of extreme expression that rarely enlightened the situation. In the case of Postville, some believed all illegal aliens should be deported and border security should be tightened dramatically. They blamed the immigrant workers for the raid and for the situation in which they found themselves. Others felt the situation was the sole responsibility of the blind greediness of American business, and the unjust and overzealous prosecution of the federal government. Protesters on both sides demonstrated at various times and locations in the months following the raid. A number of significantly large immigrant rights demonstrations were held in Iowa itself. People from around the country carried signs calling for worker rights and denouncing ICE. They joined in candlelight vigils. They wanted to *do* something. But other than making contributions to the churches and centers working with detainees' families, they could do nothing. The bitter truth was that some 400 people were experiencing firsthand the reality of federal immigration policies that are several decades old and woefully out of touch with today's global economy and rural labor shortage. All the candles and hand-made posters in the world were not going to help these Guatemalan peasants, most of whom had virtually no real understanding of why they had been arrested in the first place.

The raid brought out strong feelings from both pro- and anti-immigration camps. Many were completely unwilling to consider any element of the arguments presented by the other side, and much of the debate became mired in extremism. Talking heads on television news shows and guest opinion writers in newspapers too often resorted to emotionalism and poorly supported statistics when making their arguments. The anger and hard-line beliefs of both extremes clouded meaningful debate about what Postville meant for the rest of the country. Rancor failed to produce the kind of rational discussion that understood the need for international migrants within today's global economy and labor shortage areas, but recognized the burden this level of diversity could place on small communities poorly equipped to meet the needs of these foreign-born workers. What both sides did not want to admit is that in reality, elements of their opponents' arguments were actually valid at times, and solutions to this situation are not black and white, or quick and easy. The answers are grey and messy and complicated and have very real human and economic consequences for people of all ethnicities in towns like Postville. Our nation's unresolved immigration situation is far more complicated, murky, and multifaceted than either side realizes.

Attempts to come up with simple black-and-white solutions, such as just arresting undocumented workers or closing down the companies that employ them, often causes a host of far more complex situations that do little to address any of the real concerns expressed by either side in the immigration debate.

# CHAPTER SIX

# Diversity (The "D" Word) and Its Discontents

BECAUSE OF THE ICE RAID and its terrible human and economic toll, Postville moved to center stage in the national debate on immigration reform and globalization of the workforce. Many also look to Postville as a national social experiment for diversity and multiculturalism as it is played out in small towns and rural communities. At times we thought there were more researchers studying Postville than service providers meeting the needs of the local residents.

In a state where ethnic differences historically referred to such distinctions as Lutheran versus Catholic, Iowa has had to come a long way in its efforts to meet the needs of a rapidly changing population. Promoting tolerance and acculturation while encouraging growth and economic vitality is a challenge that's both unprecedented and enormously complex. Understanding the enormity of this challenge is central to comprehending the decline of Postville.

For years, most people who researched ethnic relations fell into one of two camps. Those who adhered to the "contact" theory believed that the more time different ethnic groups spent together, the more understanding, tolerance, and social harmony they would develop. Those who followed the "conflict" theory suggested that more contact among ethnic groups led to disputes and tension.

People who champion diversity for diversity's sake in communities or organizations assume the contact theorists are right: diverse people simply need time to get to know each other, and harmony and social cohesion will follow. Communities will benefit from greater civic engagement; the workplace will benefit from greater creativity and productivity.

These days, diversity has become a profit-making industry. It generates thousands of consulting and training companies large and small. American companies, health-care providers, and others spend billions each year on diversity training, consulting and recruitment efforts; according to one estimate, corporations annually spend as much as $8 billion on diversity training, and another $400 to $600 million on diversity consultants.

Marketing diversity like a magic bullet has caused its own set of problems. For example, several years ago one Iowa town decided that it was "too white." Town leaders and the largest local employer got together and decided that bringing diversity to their community would be an ideal way to meet the employer's labor needs. The problem was that they didn't know how to go about "getting diversity."

Some of the community's leaders had heard of Mark's work in immigration and with diversity committees around the state, so they asked him to help:

*"The evening of my visit started off well enough. About thirty of the town's key leaders were present, including the police chief, mayor, school district leaders, and others. In true Iowa fashion, people brought pizza and soft drinks by the armload. After everyone was done eating, it was my turn to make my presentation. I asked for reassurance from the audience that they wanted diversity and got resounding agreement. There was a great deal of enthusiasm in the room. The townspeople didn't want to become a meatpacking town with all of its accompanying problems*

*What followed was a pivotal moment in my career: I asked everyone to take out a piece of paper and in one or two sentences, define the term diversity. A few minutes later, when everyone had completed their assignments, I asked a few people to share their definitions. After about four people spoke, my point became obvious: everyone in the room wanted something they hadn't bothered to define; they assumed that everyone valued and understood diversity in the same way.*

*I pointed out that they had put the cart about four miles in front of the horse and needed to slow down. The crowd was unhappy; some even got angry. How dare this outsider tell them they were making a mistake? My advice was to form a subcommittee, draft a definition of diversity on their own terms, establish mission and vision statements, and outline their goals and objectives."*

Many in the room refused to thank Mark, much less shake his hand, when they left. But they had listened.

A few months later, they formed a committee to get a clearer vision of what they were after and the motivation behind it. Did they really want diversity for diversity's sake? Or was their primary goal to attract and recruit more employees, with an emphasis on nonwhite prospects? In most Iowa towns, diversity isn't invited; it just shows up, with influxes of new workers and their families. The town that was "too white" dropped most of its diversity mission when the local plant decided it didn't need so many new workers after all.

Tight-knit collections of community leaders can't be expected to understand all the complexities associated with diverse populations and workforces. These issues challenge even administrators and professionals responsible for addressing diversity issues in their communities or organizations.

Consider the focus groups Mark and Michele held in Des Moines, Iowa's capital and largest city. Most of the participants were human resource directors from major employers or local government agencies. The topic was diversity. Everyone talked about how much their company or agency valued diversity and said it was an important part of their mission. But very few of their companies had formal, written definitions of diversity, and none of the participants knew if or how their companies' diversity initiatives worked. They resorted to old affirmative-action models and outdated racial categories to measure the success of their efforts: "We have diversity: we now have three black employees and two Hispanics."

Minority diversity trainers and experts with whom we work have recounted similar stories and expressed their disappointment that success is measured by the number of nonwhites hired in a company.

Many companies and organizations share the assumption that because someone said diversity is a good thing, everybody should do it. They say there's a "business case" for diversity, citing evidence that it contributes to the bottom line by promoting creativity, productivity, and collective problem solving. They consider diversity initiatives a "strategic imperative."

These stories of the town that was "too white" and the corporations that believe in diversity are emblematic of what we have seen in so many communities, hospitals, schools, and businesses. Everyone assumes that everyone else knows what diversity is and values it. This assumption is driven in no small part by the diversity industry.

The corporate diversity business began, in part, to curtail discrimination complaints and lawsuits in the public and private sectors. Later, companies began to see it as a way to grow profits. But there's very little hard evidence that diversity initiatives contribute to the bottom line, according to diversity expert Thomas Kochan and others in the field. Kochan points out that most of the money spent on diversity training "is wasted because it is spent on programs for awareness and valuing diversity that do not give people the skills they need," such as "group processes with a focus on communicating and problem-solving in diverse teams."

Many diversity consulting and recruiting firms—as well as countless books and magazine articles on diversity—are well intentioned. But we question whether they're worth the thousands of dollars employers spend on them. Marketing the diversity business starts with building the case for diversity training and consulting in the name of social justice, which is appropriate. However, some diversity consultants can then use guilt to imply that companies and individuals are insufficiently serious about diversity if they don't sign on for (expensive) diversity training or recruiting services.

Here's the central problem with the diversity business: the people who define diversity also provide the services that help organizations achieve their diversity initiatives. This is analogous to having a dealer convince you that only one kind of car is worth buying, and then telling you the only place to buy that car is her dealership. So most organizations give in and engage diversity consultants whether they need them or not, without any assurance that the people they hire are actually qualified to serve them. A number of these trainers come from academic, government, or non-profit sectors, are highly trained, and perform their work for minimal, if any, compensation as part of their regular job duties. However, increasingly, diversity training has become a for-profit corporate venture, and others have become rich while taking advantage of organizations and communities with few resources but urgent needs in the cultural competency arena.

Also, many in the diversity business promote the idea that only "diverse" people can provide good diversity training and consultation services. All three of us have been turned down for talks or presentations, because we're white, ironically primarily by other white people working in human resource agencies. Yet, as we discuss in all our trainings, minorities will soon outnumber whites in the United States, and whites themselves will be a minority. So it is imperative that all of us, no matter what our race, learn to interact with people of different backgrounds. While we are not "people of color," we are nationally recognized for publications and trainings on cultural competency and health. Mark and Michele were recently invited to speak at a national convention about cultural competency, but the predominately white organizing committee withdrew its invitation when it learned we were white. Similarly, Aaron's "diversity" has to do with being Jewish, and an Orthodox Jew no less, and yet, he is a white, middle-aged man who grew up in the Midwest and lives and works in small-town Iowa. His presentations are met with enthusiasm and thanks, not because he talks about "diversity," but equality, opportunity, and the need to eliminate barriers for all groups, no matter what their ethnicity may be.

Another problem with the diversity business is that it is virtually unregulated, and there are few credentials or professional certification processes for practitioners. Just about anyone can be a diversity trainer or consultant. Many trainers and consultants can't demonstrate a direct link between their efforts and changes in the workplace, so there are few ways to hold them accountable. Some also focus too much on political correctness, and ignore the realities and challenges that occur with an increasingly diverse workplace. Janice Edmunds Wells, one of our favorite fellow diversity trainers and dynamic head of the Office of Multicultural Health for the state health department, is fond of telling her own Iowan audiences that while it is important to promote tolerance and cultural understanding of all ethnic groups in a worksite, it is equally imperative to set high standards, rules, and expectations for them as well.

Groups that have had a bad diversity-training experience often ask us to provide follow-up training or presentations. Sometimes these negative training experiences play on the audience's guilt about their presumed racism or religious intolerance. Sometimes people do or say things that make them uncomfortable and that lead to the opposite of what trainers say they are after: a new appreciation for "otherness." For instance, Mark now trains new state patrol troopers in Iowa. His predecessor told the trainees—within the first five minutes of his presentation—that they were "all racist." We've all followed up with people who were traumatized when diversity trainers forced them to use racist slurs that had never crossed their lips before. Indeed, in some cases, their negative experiences with diversity training could come right out of a painfully honest episode of the television show "The Office." Often trainers instruct people to hug each other, stare into one another's eyes, or tell their fellow attendees how much they mean to them. We call this "Kumbayah" training, nothing more than a song. Many people we meet were humiliated during their diversity training; some were angry and resentful. Most felt they weren't treated as individuals, but were stereotyped themselves by the trainers and other audience members. We've lost count of the times we've entered a training room and immediately sensed participants' resentment. They're clearly thinking, "*Why* do we have to go through more diversity training?"

There is a profound split in the intercultural training and education field. On one side are those who believe you have to change people's attitudes before you can change their behavior. On the other side are those who say trying to change people's feelings is a waste of time; instead, you should focus on behavioral change.

In the former camp are those who often play on shame or guilt. We've heard them make outrageous statements such as "Only white people can be racist," or "Deep inside, all Jews hate themselves." These statements themselves are racist and hateful.

Members of the latter camp, the trainers who focus on behavior, believe people shouldn't have to apologize for who they are, but must be aware of what they do and say to others. These trainers recognize that people resent being told there is something inherently wrong with them. But education and training can help them better understand others and behave in a more culturally aware and sensitive manner.

Much of the information disseminated at diversity trainings and presentations—as well as by the media, of course—is wrong or misleading. Often training sessions reflect the presenters' biases. For this reason, our post-training sessions emphasize that many people are uninformed or misinformed, not *ignorant*, when it comes to diversity issues.

When people are uninformed or misinformed about others, they are prone to accept generalizations—statements about a population based on some kind of statistical measure—as facts that apply to every individual. For example, based on statistical information, it is reasonable to make the statement that most Americans speak only one language, English. But to presume that a U.S. citizen speaks only English is to stereotype that person.

This commentary on diversity education is certainly relevant to the case of Postville. In this little town and other communities, we often battle misinformation about ethnic groups: Latinos ("they are all in the country illegally," "they don't want to learn English," "they don't pay taxes," etc.); Jews ("you meet one Jew, you've met them all," "all of the Jews in Postville are from New York," "Jews don't use banks and they always pay with cash so they can hide their incomes"); and local whites ("they are cold-hearted," "they are all racists," "the Iowans are very narrow-minded and hate foreigners").

Responding to these stereotypes informs our experience in Postville. Because we live and work there, we see Postville as a sum of its many parts. We see it as a living, breathing, dynamic community that has shown a remarkable resilience despite all of the controversy and international media attention. But to outsiders, Postville is an undiscovered country, an inexplicable place filled with strange people who do strange things. All three of us encounter—almost on a daily basis—people's fascination with and curiosity about the town. When we mention that we live or work there, people greet us with looks of utter astonishment.

Sometimes we need a good deal of patience—not to deal with people's questions about Postville, but to withstand their presumptions. Many people boil down the town's complex situation to one simple question: "Does diversity work?" How can we answer this question while passing someone in the grocery store? Yet even some professionals, who should understand that most issues are complicated, often look for the "elevator talk" about Postville.

Many of the ideas people have about Postville, and much of the language they use—and expect us to use when we describe our lives or work there—come straight out of the diversity business. The industry has imposed the idea of "celebrating" diversity on Postville and other communities around the country.

People see in Postville what they want to see. If they see something they *don't* want to see, they discount it. As a Postville resident, Aaron encounters many people who briefly visit the community, bring their own language and assumptions to describe what they see, and go away to talk about it. Aaron calls these people "carpetbaggers." Like many of his fellow residents, he has grown weary of being judged by outsiders who can't begin to understand the joys and tribulations of life in a diverse, under-resourced, rural American town.

&#10148;&#8226;&#10124;

There are as many perspectives on Postville as there are residents and groups within the community. For example, some outsiders view the community only through the lens of the Latinos that live there. In their view, the Latinos are seen as exploited migrants that are forced to come to the United States because of poverty in their own countries and are victims of American capitalism and corporate greed. Others sympathize only with the local white Christians in town and understand why they might feel threatened by the Jews who moved into Postville. After all, the Jews didn't play by the rules, cut their grass, or share their food. In the beginning, they didn't even know how to drive! To them, the Jews are a puzzle at best and destructive at worst, what with their intolerance and determination to maintain their separate identities at the expense of the locals. Even others feel sorry for the Jews, primarily those from the East Coast, and pity them for having to work and live in the cultural wasteland of the rural Midwest while backwards anti-Semites run amuck around them.

Narrow, overly simplistic, stereotyped perspectives like those just described are ridiculous and just plain wrong. Unfortunately, they are also all too common. These views demonstrate the need for a greater, in-depth understanding of the reality of life for people in towns like Postville. In many ways, life and their experiences vary dramatically within each of the subcultures that may inhabit these small communities. In reality, though, these groups usually share even more similarities than differences and actually have a much richer level of symbiosis and synergy with each other than outsiders could ever understand. The shallowness of the stereotypes of each cultural group in town, whether it be Jews, Latinos, local white Christians, or others, simply reflects the inanity of political correctness and the rhetoric of the professional diversity industry. It's fair enough to talk about the challenges Postville faced as new populations came to town. It's absurdly *un*fair to for outsiders to make assumptions about how people perceive each other or interact with these communities.

For years, we witnessed hardworking, well-meaning Postville residents trying to make diversity work in their town. But it often seemed as if Postville had to live up to someone else's definition of diversity. Everything the town did was judged by people outside the community with their own standards for the town's success. At one time, people constantly asked us to talk about Postville as a model for diversity. When things changed and the town was no longer considered a Shangri-La, people only wanted us to talk about its failures.

Making diversity work in a town like Postville takes time, patience, and hard labor. When outsiders use their own criteria to decide whether a town has succeeded or failed, they do the community a vast disservice.

Earlier in this chapter we discussed the two competing theories of ethnic relations: "conflict" versus "contact." Harvard political scientist Robert Putnam has conducted research that contradicts both of these theories. Putnam wrote the acclaimed 2000 book *Bowling Alone*, about the decline of civic engagement in America. In his more recent research, he focused on nearly 30,000 people in diverse communities across the U.S. He found that levels of trust and civic engagement decline as diversity increases. Yet he insists these challenges can be overcome. Given this country's tremendous and rapid ethnic diversification, he had better be right.

Like us, Putnam is a realist. When he published his findings, he worried that people would read into them what they wanted to read, just as people see in Postville what they want to see. "It would be unfortunate if a politically correct progressivism were to deny the reality of the challenge to social solidarity posed by diversity," he wrote. "It would be equally unfortunate if an ahistorical and ethnocentric conservatism were to deny that addressing the challenge is both feasible and desirable."

Perhaps the most poignant reminder of Postville's history is the story of the town's Diversity Garden. Several years ago, the extension service at Iowa State University started a community garden program. The agent working in northeast Iowa established a wonderful garden near Postville's northern border. To honor the town's unique situation, she decided to call it the Diversity Garden. Immigrants and long-time residents alike began tending plots and growing their own food in the garden. The extension service and other agencies provided seeds and tools.

For several years, people carefully maintained the plots. The academic extension service declared the garden a success and an example of how diversity can work in rural Iowa. But then the garden fell into neglect; the majority of plots were left unworked and unweeded. The Diversity Garden was no more. In other words, as long as someone could take credit for the garden's success, it was a success. When it failed, no one wanted to be associated with it, and few would provide the technical assistance or support to help keep it going.

As one Postville resident is fond of saying, "What looks good is good. What looks bad is really a good that is hidden." This is how we like to think about the community garden and Postville. From the weeds, someday people will again grow food for their families. And from what happened in Postville, some hidden good will emerge.

Ultimately, the town's success won't be judged by outsiders with their politically correct notions of success, the media that profits from the town's difficulties, or the naysayers who impose their own prejudices on the community. Only the people of Postville—white, black, Latino, Jew, and Christian alike—should define what hidden good will come from their struggles.

# CHAPTER SEVEN

# Cain vs. Abel

THOSE IN THE DIVERSITY BUSINESS often over-look one crucial fact: people are *individuals*. Within any given group, people differ tremendous-ly; the shared ethnicity of a certain population may be less important than factors such as class, gender, age, birthplace, religion, family of origin, and person-al behaviors.

Postville has been home to dozens of different ethnic groups over the past decade or two, each com-prised of diverse individuals. For instance, the suppos-edly monolithic Latino population has included immigrants from Mexico, El Salvador, Guatemala, Ar-gentina, and other nations; Catholics, Protestants, Evangelicals, Jews, and non-believers; peasants, teach-ers, rabbis, social workers, and interpreters. Even those from the same country, such as Mexico, are more like-ly to identify themselves by their home towns or states than by their nation of origin. And so the story goes for all groups in Postville, including Africans, Eastern Europeans, Jews, and white locals.

"The Jews" in Postville offer a prime example of the diversity within diversity. Traditionally, Jews have been Postville's second largest population, right after the local Christians. At times, the town of 2,000 or so people has included 300 Jews. Jews have come from all over the world to work in Postville. Many are citizens of the United States, born in places such as New York or New Jersey or California. Others come from Israel, Poland, Russia, Lithuania, Argentina, or other nations. Some speak English as their native language; for others, it's Hebrew or Yiddish. Some are Orthodox Jews; some are non-observant secular Israelis. Even the Orthodox Jews come from half dozen or more sects. Some are well educated and work as doctors, lawyers, nurses, accountants, or teachers. Others specialize in the vocational trade of ritual kosher slaughtering. The list of differences goes on and on, just as it does among Postville's white Christian residents. There is no monolithic Jewish community in Postville, or anywhere else in the world.

Agriprocessors and Postville's Jewish community were mired in controversy even before ICE's raid. In 2004 and 2008, People for the Ethical Treatment of Animals sent undercover supporters into the plant to film the slaughter of cattle. PETA then put the footage on its website. Out of the hundreds of cows killed at the plant in the days the operatives filmed, PETA chose to show the footage of some cows that didn't die immediately. The videos also showed instances in which the *shochet*, the specially trained rabbi, made secondary cuts into cows' throats after the initial cut to better vent the blood.

In non-kosher industrial beef plants, most cattle are killed by a process called knocking or stunning. As each cow comes into the factory, a worker holds a metal cylinder to its forehead. The cylinder contains a metal rod about three inches long. This rod is propelled into the cow's head with tremendous force, powered by a .22-caliber bullet shell. The cow dies instantly. In other plants, workers use electric shock to stop the cow's heart. Other plants break the cow's neck.

In kosher plants, the laws of *shechita*, or ritual slaughter, dictate how animals are to be killed. The *shochet* must cut through the cow's neck and its main artery in one quick, smooth motion. At the Postville plant, cows were herded into a large machine that grabbed each animal, turned it upside down, and exposed the neck. A rabbi then approached the animal with a long, extremely sharp silver knife and cut the cow's neck. Blood flew everywhere. In non-kosher plants, workers don't cut the neck, because they want to drain and keep the blood. But in kosher production, the meat must be devoid of blood. The cow's blood is rendered with all of the other unusable by-products.

Informed consumers of kosher meat know full well how animals are slaughtered. But the PETA videos focused on the fact that not all cows die immediately during the ritual slaughter and showed the animals suffering and struggling. The videos upset and angered some Jews; humane ritual kosher slaughter is supposed to ensure that animals don't suffer. Of course, many non-Jews were upset as well.

Some incensed Jews pointed out that Hitler banned *shechita* and criticized the practice to demonize Jews and promote their marginalization (and eventual murder) under the Nazi regime. Many Jews were especially appalled when, in 2003, PETA launched its "Holocaust on a Plate" campaign, which compared the slaughter of cows and chickens to the slaughter of Jews and others in the Nazi death camps. (PETA co-founder Ingrid Newkirk once said, "Six million Jews died in concentration camps, but six billion broiler chickens will die this year in slaughterhouses.") Equating the Holocaust with the meat industry was bound to offend almost everyone, but it also got PETA a lot of attention. Many Jews and non-Jews alike were upset by PETA's insistence that humans and animals have the same moral standing.

*National Geographic* used the PETA controversy as a springboard for a short article about Postville in June 2005. The magazine quoted Shalom Rubashkin: "'I think PETA is after the shechita process,' he says in a staccato Brooklyn accent that has not softened after years in the Midwest. 'They'd love to make it illegal.'" The author framed the PETA videos within the familiar Jews-versus-locals controversy. But in the end, the piece recognized how far Postville had come: "Rubashkin says his people have simply learned to fit in. They invite neighbors to their bar mitzvahs and have grown to appreciate a mowed lawn . . . . Now that PETA has targeted Agriprocessors—a threat from true outsiders—the town has rallied round. The city council passed a resolution renouncing 'unfounded and unproven attacks on Agriprocessors, Inc. or its kosher processing.' "

※-※

The debate about the PETA footage reflected some of the traditional divides among Jews—the same divisions that appeared after the ICE raid. As we noted earlier, there is no such thing as a monolithic Jewish community, just as there is no monolithic Christian, white, black, or Latino community. Like all populations, Jews are diverse and heterogeneous.

Jews may be of *Ashkenazi* descent—primarily of white European heritage, or of *Sephardic* descent—from Hispanic or Middle Eastern countries. Jews also fall into one of three broadly defined religious movements. Reform Jews tend to be the most liberal and least observant; few keep kosher or observe the Sabbath. Conservative Jews are somewhat more observant and have more traditional views of Jewish teachings and practices. Orthodox Jews are the most conservative and follow the strictest interpretation of Judaism. Hassidic Jews are sometimes referred to as ultra-Orthodox Jews because they take religious conservatism several steps further. They generally choose to live among themselves. They dress in traditional clothing, follow strict kosher food and lifestyle practices, deeply honor the Sabbath, and practice sexual modesty and gender segregation. Most Jews in Postville belong to this group.

After the PETA videos appeared, most Jews reacted in one of three ways, reflecting the three broadly defined Jewish movements described above. Many Reform Jews considered the PETA exposé further justification for not buying or consuming kosher meat. To them, the slaughter practice was further evidence of the backward, out-of-touch lifestyle of the Orthodox Jews (who, in turn, tend to think the Reform Jews aren't real practicing Jews).

Some Conservative rabbis expressed concern about the PETA tapes, and some even called for a boycott of Agri meat. In response, Orthodox critics said the Conservative Jews were trying to get back into the kosher certification business, which is dominated by Orthodox groups.

The Conservative call to boycott Agri had little effect, and the whole PETA controversy settled down somewhat in 2006, when the plant was approved by a well-known authority on humane slaughter practices. In 2008, more PETA footage emerged. But by then there were already calls for Agri boycotts because of ICE raid and subsequent issues.

In 2006, an article in the *Jewish Daily Forward*—an East Coast newspaper aimed mainly at Reform Jews as well as some Conservative Jews—ignited controversy about Agri's treatment of its labor force. The article described the plant as a "Kosher Jungle," alluding to Upton Sinclair's gut-wrenching account of meatpacking plants in the early twentieth century.

The *Forward* exposé, which relied on interviews with several workers, described harsh working conditions in the Agri plant and suggested that the plant didn't adhere to broader interpretations of *Kashrut* law regarding ethical practices. The article set off a debate among Jews about whether they should boycott Agri products.

After the article appeared, a number of rabbis from various Jewish groups visited the plant. The Orthodox rabbi—who was also a member of the Chabad-Lubavitch movement—found nothing amiss. On a separate visit, the Conservative rabbi criticized the plant but didn't call for a formal boycott of Agri products.

The issue of *Kashrut* and worker treatment opened up some old battle lines among Jews. Herein lies another of the forces at work in Postville: Orthodox Jews, particularly those in the Chabad movement, were more likely to "circle the wagons" when responding to outside threats, whether from the media, non-Jews, or even other less conservative Jews, Reform and Conservative Jews were more likely to open the topic for debate. As the *Forward* put it, "These rifts have been particularly sharp in the rabbinate, where the terms of debate are not abstract questions but matters of their own moral standing."

The May 2008 ICE raid reignited the debate about hiring and mistreating vulnerable workers at the plant. Fissures that appeared in 2006 gaped after the raid. Some Jewish groups in the U.S. immediately called for a boycott of Agri products. Some, particularly fellow Orthodox groups, took an innocent-until-proven-guilty approach. Others denounced the allegations against Agri as just another form of anti-Semitism.

After extensive coverage of worker abuse in addition to new allegations of child labor violations in the plant, the many sides in the kosher debate hardened their stances, and the debate raged in the Jewish media. Arguments were particularly intense on the controversial website failedmessiah.com. The blog is run by Shmarya Rosenberg, a former Lubavitcher who is now a secular Jew and one of the most ardent critics of Chabad and Orthodox Judaism. Rosenberg is a folk hero among many liberal Jews; because of his reporting, he has been recognized as one of the Fifty Most Influential Jews by publications such as the *Forward*. However, many Orthodox Jews felt that his controversial blog did more than just pass along information about the Postville raid. At times, they said, he seemed to suggest that he was acting as Postville's guardian, looking out for the town when no one else seemed to be doing so. The situation became even more heated when Shmaryia Rosenberg assisted Radio Postville in its emergency relief efforts after the raid; many Orthodox Jews felt he was sensationalizing the crisis.

❧•❧

The debate among Jews was not just about morals and ethics. It was also about maintaining Agriprocessors' certification as a kosher food producer. Without kosher certification, the plant would lose its tremendous share of the kosher meat market—and quite possibly go out of business.

Allegations about poor working conditions at Agri had raged for years. On top of the brutal nature of the job itself, there were reports of mistreatment, sexual harassment, physical and verbal attacks by supervisors, and other incidents. Workers complained to local churches and social service providers. Some said they were dismissed after a serious injury; others said they were fired after taking an attitude with their boss. Rumors spread about underage workers. And then, of course, there were rumors about illegal immigrants, including much speculation about how they got the papers they needed to be hired.

Many of these allegations became federal indictments and convictions after the 2008 ICE raid. A woman who worked in the Agri human resources department pleaded guilty to one count of conspiracy to harbor undocumented aliens and one count of aggravated identity theft. She faced up to twelve years in prison. Another member of the Agri human resources department pleaded guilty to a misdemeanor charge of aiding and abetting a pattern or practice of knowingly hiring undocumented immigrants. One Latino supervisor, who was in charge of the beef line, pleaded guilty to conspiracy to hire illegal aliens and aiding and abetting the hiring of illegal aliens. Another Latino supervisor pled guilty to one count of aiding and abetting the harboring of undocumented immigrants.

Major charges were handed down to the plant's vice president, Shalom Rubashkin, and other administrators. The charges included hiring sixteen underage workers and exposing them to dangerous machines and dangerous chemicals. Rubashkin also was indicted on multiple accounts for conspiracy to harbor undocumented workers for profit, harboring and aiding and abetting the harboring of undocumented workers for profit, conspiracy to commit document fraud, aiding and abetting document fraud, bank fraud, and money laundering.

Unfortunately, the allegations about worker mistreatment are hardly unique to Agriprocessors and are all too common among other meatpacking and agricultural processing companies. (The charges also had nothing to do with fact that the owners were Jewish, although the religion of the plant operators was usually cited in most media reports.) The plant experienced turnover among rabbis, too; some of them even went on strike a few months after the raid to protest salary irregularities.

Yet we found ourselves facing awkward questions from outside observers, including the outsiders that Aaron so often resents and refers to as "carpetbaggers": How much worker mistreatment, both before and after, the raid, could be accounted for by the Jewish owners' bias against their non-Jewish, highly marginalized workers? Was Agri just another mismanaged packing plant, or did the plant's owners exploit and abuse its immigrant workers *because* they were immigrants? Did management believe they had some religious justification for viewing the plant's workforce as disposable?

As some of the Jews discussed quietly, alleged worker abuse may not have been directed solely to immigrant workers. Ironically, they noted that

Rubashkin and some of his managers were just as abusive toward Jewish employees as they were toward non-Jews. Rabbis often went without pay for several weeks, and Jewish workers were treated with no more respect than anyone else. (In general, Rubashkin had a reputation being fair and even generous, but in the plant—where there was so much pressure to get animals in one door and product out the other—all bets were off.)

Jews and others will argue about these issues for years to come. A number of Postville Jews sense that they are culturally different not only from the *goyim* but from other Jews as well. Some less observant Jews harshly criticize Orthodox Hasidic Jews for many of their practices and consider them judgmental and arrogant for segregating themselves from those who have different beliefs, don't work hard enough at their spirituality, or don't follow the same "rules" for practicing religion.

When the national group Jewish Community Action (JCA), which is made up mostly of liberal Jews, began paying close attention to Postville in recent years in light of the PETA scandal and other concerns, many of the town's Orthodox Jews were dismayed. Among other things, JCA sponsored Dr. Camayd's well-attended appearance at the synagogue in St. Paul and participated in large pro-immigration rallies in Postville. Orthodox Jews argued back, and asked: Why didn't JCA care about the plight of Postville workers before the raid? Did they express concern after the raid merely to underscore their differences with the Orthodox? Would the group care about the Postville workers if they didn't work in a kosher plant?

Regardless of the inter-Jewish debates that raged on, many people wrongly assumed that all the Jews in Postville either co-owned or managed the plant. Most Jewish men in town did work at or otherwise depended on Agri for their livelihood. But the plant wasn't owned by a collective of Jews; it was owned privately by one family, the Rubashkins.

Since most Jews in Postville depended on the plant, they also depended on the Rubashkin family. The Rubashkins were rightly credited with building the infrastructure that made Jewish life possible in Postville, such as the *shul* and Jewish schools. The local Jewish community was grateful for the economic opportunities the Agri plant afforded them.

Indeed, of all the immigrant groups in town, Jews were—and remain—most vested in the community. Many have homes and mortgages, large numbers of children, and other ties to the "shtetl on the prairie." They thrived in the community the Rubashkins helped build. The Jews appreciated what the Rubashkins contributed to Postville, but that doesn't mean they agreed with or respected everything the Rubashkins did.

A number of Jews in Postville now openly admit their concerns about how the Rubashkins operated the plant, and question the family's business tactics. At the same time, some Jews, whether they be Reform or Orthodox, believe the ICE raid and subsequent charges had anti-Semitic undertones to it. For example, they ask: why didn't ICE and the government force detainees in the Mississippi raid, which occurred two months after Postville, to plead guilty to felony charges? Unlike Postville's detainees, those in Mississippi faced deportation rather than prison. They ask another question: if hiring illegal immigrants is prevalent in the meatpacking industry, why was the Agri boss the only meatpacking senior manager arrested and charged with hiring illegal immigrants?

Some Jews outside Postville used the term *pogrom* to describe the assault on Agri and the Rusbashkins. But Postville Jews, many of whom are the children of Holocaust survivors themselves, know this is a stretch. Postville may be a kind of metaphorical shtetl, but the federal government is no Cossack gang riding over the hill to wipe it out. Privately, some Postville Jews still give Rubashkin the benefit of the doubt and chose to reserve judgment until Rubashkin's trials end. But as Aaron is fond of saying, if Rubashkin is convicted after a just trial, no Torah-observant Jew will find his behavior acceptable.

# CHAPTER EIGHT

# Meanwhile, Back at the Shtetl: One Year After the Raid

THE YEAR FOLLOWING THE ICE RAID was marked by economic and social decline, a dramatic loss of population, and several important developments in the Agriprocessors situation. It was a year full of uncertainty and apprehension for everyone in Postville. By May 2009, Postville lost 40 percent of its pre-raid population, the economy was in shambles, the city government teetered on the brink of financial collapse, and the future the town's major employer grew increasingly doubtful with time.

With its workforce decimated by the ICE raid, Agriprocessors was forced to find a new, legal workforce. As noted in an earlier chapter, to do so, the company contracted with three employment recruitment agencies, one from Iowa, one from Texas and one from the East Coast. The Iowa-based company, Jacobson Staffing, also became the plant's *de facto* human resources department, and they set up offices next to the Agri plant. The labor recruitment efforts began in earnest in July 2008 and reached their peak in November. For these few months, Postville experienced several waves of newcomers from across the United States and abroad. Most of the U.S. citizens were unemployed, down-on-their-luck types with few prospects for employment other than jobs no one else wanted. They included homeless people, people recently released from prison, recovering drug addicts and others.

The arrival of these transients in particular put the town on edge, and this was reflected in crime statistics. The eight months following the raid were particularly unsettled. During the four months prior to May 2008, Postville police averaged only about six adult arrests and eleven disturbance calls per month. During the same time period, there were only two total assaults, one public intoxication, and no arrests for disorderly conduct. However, during the eight months from May through December 2008, Postville police averaged nearly sixteen adult arrests (including one arrest for attempted murder in Texas) and sixteen disturbance calls per month. Assaults increased, and there were even a handful of arrests for weapons charges. The situation peaked from September to November, 2008. In September, there were twenty-three adult arrests, with twenty in October and twenty-two in November. Things were so unsettled that the Postville police added an extra shift during these three months and called for assistance from the Iowa State Patrol and the county sheriff's office periodically. On Friday nights, four or five officers were on duty during this time.

After the trouble makers were fired or quit working at Agri and the bitter Iowa winter began in earnest, things began to settle down again, and crime rates went back to their pre-raid levels. Indeed, between January and April 2009, there were only two total arrests for assault, an average of only ten disturbance calls per month, and only about seven adult arrests per month. Public intoxication and disorderly conduct charges dropped to virtually none.

Growth in transient populations and crime rates also impacted local ambulance services. Prior to the ICE raid, the ambulance service in Postville averaged between fifteen and twenty "runs" per month. After the raid—and particularly between September and November of 2008—they averaged thirty to thirty-five runs per month. The additional runs were usually associated with drunkenness, fights, and existing medical conditions among transients from out of state. As a private, non-profit agency that contracts with Postville and nearby communities, the area ambulance service depends on private payments and insurance reimbursements to meet its budget. But for the first time, the service lost revenue because of the number of runs it provided to transient patients who did not pay or who had no health insurance to cover the costs. For an ambulance service that operated on an annual approximate budget of $100,000, the unpaid runs presented the service with a deficit of more than $25,000 in less than four months.

Many of the U.S. citizen and foreign-born people brought to Postville by the recruiting firms did not work very long in the plant, saw their paychecks dwindle with payments to recruiters for "conveyance" and other fees, and most were not provided return transportation to their points of origin. Many literally did not have enough money to return home, and most of these folks were forced to ask for assistance with bus tickets and related needs from St. Bridget's church and other organizations in town.

Throughout the year after the ICE raid, Postville saw its total Latino population decline sharply with most of the Guatemalan arrestees either imprisoned, deported back home, or gone to other meatpacking towns. It was particularly ironic that the core Latino community that remained in Postville was made up mostly of fifty-six people arrested by ICE on identity theft charges, but later released on humanitarian grounds to take care of young children or for health reasons. Several minors were also released. Among the adults allowed to stay in Postville, ICE fitted most of them with GPS ankle monitoring equipment. These devices could not be taken off their legsand had to be plugged in two hours each day to be recharged. In some cases, they overheated and burned detainees' skin. These people were left in Postville, but were not allowed to work or leave Iowa until the government decided if they would be used as material witnesses in a litany of felony charges against the plant owner, Shalom Rubashkin. So, the migrant workers became entirely dependent on St. Bridget's church and other town organizations like the food bank for survival.

Thanks to frequent, concerned national exposure by media of the dire situation for these detainees caught in legal limbo in Postville, donations to St. Bridget's were tremendous. Indeed, one year after the raid, the church announced that it had received private donations from forty-nine of the fifty states, amounting to more than $1 million. Total state government aid in cash amounted to only $698,000, which was primarily in the form of a one-time grant from the Iowa Department of Economic Development's homeless program to pay for rent and utilities for the displaced, although the Governor's office assigned several young VISTA volunteers to work out of Postville with recovery efforts. It was not lost on anyone in Postville or the media that no financial relief or grant assistance was provided directly to Postville from the federal government, and written pleas for assistance to various agencies were denied.

A few months after the raid, St. Bridget's learned that the federal government intended to bring to Postville some thirty people who were going to be released from prison as material witnesses in the case against Agriprocessors, but they, too, would be given GPS ankle monitors and not allowed to work. Local relief agencies were angry with the prospect of having even more people to feed, more rents to pay, more families to care for, and no funding from the state or federal government, and they viewed this situation as even further collateral damage wrought by the ICE raid. They knew that millions had been spent on the raid, detaining the prisoners in Waterloo and elsewhere around the country, and pursuing an astonishing array of charges against the owners, but not a dime was spent to sustain the detainees and witnesses dumped at Postville's doorstep. Most were not even given the opportunity to earn a living, which, ironically, they could have had by working at the Agri plant which desperately needed their labor.

The inability of the recruiting firms to enlist a sufficient number of new legal workers, and the high turnover and transience among those who did arrive, meant that the Agri plant never got back to full operation. There were a few demonstrations of the beef slaughter process for prospective buyers of the plant, but the beef line never ran again. Several months after the raid, there were numerous unsubstantiated reports that the beef part of the plant had been severely damaged by a water main break and would take a significant investment of resources to get it running properly again. But a key employee at Agri assured us there was no truth in these rumors. As he told us, "this is story has no legs."

The plant struggled to staff and maintain only one line to slaughter and process chickens and turkeys. This limited production provided insufficient cash flow. Frustrated by decreased and intermittent pay by Agri after the ICE raid, some fifty Jewish rabbis who worked at Agri temporarily walked off the job on August 21, 2008.

Agriprocessors filed for Chapter 11 bankruptcy protection in November 2008, citing the effects of the ICE raid. The plant owed nearly $100 million to hundreds of creditors. One of their largest debts was to one of the recruiting companies hired to restaff the plant with legal workers. Creditors also include several local businesses that may or may not see the money owed them by Agri. The bankruptcy was another massive blow to the local regional economy.

With the bankruptcy filing, Agriprocessors was placed under a trustee whose job was to get the plant running again and then sell it. Rumors spread like wildfire about potential imminent buyers from the United States and abroad. The Israeli food producer Soglowek publicly declared interest in buying the plant, but it later withdrew its offer. The property formally went to auction in late March 2009. The number of bidders and the value of their bids were disappointing. The highest bid was only $15 million, well below the $30 million demanded by the banks holding the Agri's debt. There were also a number of concerns and questions about origins of some of the companies bidding on the sale. There were many concerns in the media and in the blogosphere that some of the bidders were elaborate fronts for the Rubashkins. In any case, the auction failed, and the trustee was left trying to find more potential buyers. The possibility loomed that the plant would be broken up and sold in pieces. If that happened and the plant closed down permanently, Postville would continue its painful slide into economic and social decline, with no reasonable prospect for recovery.

Even for months after the failed bankruptcy auction, there were still new rumors daily about potential buyers. There was a bright spot in early May 2009 when an investor from Montreal bought a $10 million line of credit for the plant, and several sources told the media that a sale was imminent. On May 22, the bankruptcy trustees told the media an announcement of the plant's sale would be issued "shortly." Weeks later, it still hadn't happened. Again, speculation ran rampant in the blogosphere that the deal was being held up because the potential buyer had ties to questionable business deals. Insiders felt the delay probably had more to do with the complexity of negotiations with the multiple creditors involved.

In March 2009, Rubashkin's Nevel Properties filed for bankruptcy protection as well. It owed money to local banks, utility providers, and the City of Postville, among others. The other major housing company in town, GAL Investments, did not formally file for bankruptcy, but GAL and Nevel both saw their businesses collapse in light of lack of renters. Prior to the raid, GAL generated monthly revenue of $192,000. A year later, just nineteen of GAL's 129 rental units were occupied, and the company took in only $16,000 in April 2009. Similar occupancy rates were found among Nevel properties. Ironically, though, the financial collapse of these housing companies brought further economic devastation to the community. By May 2009, "For Sale by Owner" posters and signs from real estate agents were found throughout the community. House values plummeted, exacerbated by the fact that when the town was thriving and renters were abundant, Nevel and GAL engaged in small bidding wars for property, jacking up sales prices well above what the houses are worth today. Of some 700 houses in Postville, 228 were for sale in

May 2009. Some of these homes were also put on the market by large Jewish families leaving town for better prospects elsewhere.

The loss of jobs and people also meant steep losses in taxes and utility revenue. By May 2009, Nevel Properties alone owed $95,000. Agri owed more than $250,000 in property taxes. Sales taxes were also off by 27 percent and declining with the loss of downtown businesses. Prior to the raid, Postville used to bill about $92,000 each month for water, sewage and garbage service. By May 2009, the city was only receiving about $60,000 for these services. The result was that the renters and home owners who remained in Postville were forced to make up the difference, and their city utility bills increased by 35 percent. The utility situation would have been much worse if it not been for the infusion of funds from the state to help pay for rent and utilities. But when that money ran out in about March 2009, the city got hammered with unpaid bills. As a result, the city placed dozens of utility leans on GAL, Nevel and other properties in Postville, although Nevel eventually caught up with its water bills after filing for bankruptcy.

Agriprocessors' bankruptcy also meant that the plant no longer made payments for its $10 million waste water treatment plant. The city built the lagoon with funding from the U.S. Department of Agriculture with an agreement that Agri would help pay for the facility and eventually take control. Alas, Agri did not keep up its payments for the lagoon. Initially, the U.S.D.A. turned down the city's appeal for a one-year deferral of payments. This left the city scrambling to find some way to make the semi-annual payment of $167,000. But after June 1, 2009, the U.S.D.A. starting working with the city to work up a flexible, workable schedule for repayment.

Late July 2008 saw a massive demonstration protest march in Postville. The principle issues at hand were unjust immigration policies and how massive workplace raids have dire consequences for communities like Postville. Some 1,000 people attended a service at St. Bridget's church and then marched to the Agri plant. A large number of marchers from several states joined the march. People chanted in Spanish and English such sayings as "Yes we can" and "A people united can never be divided." The raid was still quite fresh in the media, and that, no doubt, led several counter protestors to arrive for the march. As many as 100 of these pro-raid people lined the sidewalks, some holding signs that read "Go Home!," "Save the American Worker," or "What Would Jesus Do? Obey the Law!"

The march was organized by St. Bridget's, other churches in Postville, Jewish Community Action from the Twin Cities, and the Jewish Council on Urban Affairs from Chicago. The active role of these two Jewish organizations was born mostly of their desire to advocate for humane treatment of immigrants and the need to support immigration reform and migrant rights. But many Postville Jews felt their actions were detrimental and insensitive. Indeed, a reporter for the Postville newspaper wrote, "Several hundred of the walkers were Jewish people who wanted to demonstrate their disapproval of the happenings at Agriprocessors." Many Postville Jews found the march to the Agri plant ironic: if the real issue at stake was to show solidarity with those affected by the ICE raid, why condemn a plant that just lost its workforce, including many Jews, and could no longer provide kosher meat products to thousands of Jewish consumers around the world dependent on their products? The debate between the various Jewish movements was endless on this issue.

During the court proceedings at the Waterloo Cattle Congress, 302 of the Postville detainees were forced into a plea bargain agreement: they would not be charged with felony aggravated identity theft, if they pled guilty to lesser charges of using a false Social Security number and accepted a five-month jail sentence and subsequent deportation. As we explained in an earlier chapter, these arrangements met with howls of protest in the legal community and within immigration advocacy circles. The irony is that if the raid had taken place one year later, the plea agreement arranged by the federal court in Waterloo could not have happened. On May 4, 2009, the U.S. Supreme Court unanimously ruled that prosecutors should not charge immigrants with aggravated identity theft unless the prosecutors can prove the immigrants *knowingly* used Social Security numbers or other forms of identifications that belonged to actual people. Prosecutors in the Postville case never considered the level of knowledge the arrestees had about the origin of their fraudulent identification to gain employment, but nonetheless the detainees found themselves rapidly convicted on aggravated identity theft-related charges. Indeed, most of the detainees were not even aware that they needed a Social Security number to work in the U.S., and they did not know that the numbers and identities they were using may have belonged to real people. They were primarily Guatemalan peasants with extremely low literacy and education levels, even in their own languages, let alone in English. While many knew they were working in the United States without proper authority (a relatively minor administrative law violation), most did not know that the illegal work documents they were using had Social Security numbers on them that were stolen or bought from American citizens (a serious felony). As Justice Stephen G. Breyer wrote in the court's decision, "As a matter of ordinary English grammar, it seems natural to read the statute's word 'knowingly' as applying to all the subsequently listed elements of the crime."

Those concerned about what happened to the Postville detainees praised the decision. For these detainees, the majority of whom had already served their jail terms and had been deported, the court's decision came too late. But, the decision will have a major impact on how the government prosecutes immigrant identity cases in the future. Many in Postville felt the Supreme Court ruling vindicated their contention that the ICE raid was purposefully exaggerated and used excessive force.

Although the Supreme Court's decision didn't help the Postville detainees, it did have an immediate impact on other defendants in the Agriprocessors case. Laura Althouse, who pled guilty to aggravated

identity-theft and conspiracy to harbor undocumented immigrants for financial gain in October 2008 immediately requested to withdraw her guilty plea to
the identity-theft charge. Prosecutors did not object.
She remained guilty of the harboring charges, and,
as of May 2009, she had not yet been sentenced.

In light of the Supreme Court decision, Shalom
Rubashkin also requested to have seven identity theft
charges against him, Brent Beebe, and two others dismissed. The irony is that these charges were dropped,
but at the same time an additional seventy charges
were made. By May 2009, Rubashkin, Beebe and the
two others—who reportedly fled to Israel—faced a
total of 142 felony charges.

⇜ ⇝

The one-year anniversary of the ICE raid in
Postville was marked by a several events. First was the
ringing of church bells 397 times, once for each person arrested during the raid. Someone at the Yeshiva
also blew a *shofar* horn in honor of the detainees.
There was a Prayer Service at St. Bridget's Church with
a printed program in English, Spanish and Hebrew.
Several people spoke, including Christian priests and
pastors, and Jewish Rabbis. The name of each detainee
was read aloud. A march then took place from the
church to Agriprocessors. Media emerged from
throughout the Midwest, and, once again, satellite
trucks lined Postville streets. In an ironic twist, the
media were specifically asked to not arrive via helicopter because of the trauma people experienced with

helicopters during the ICE raid. Yet, about ten minutes before the prayer service started, a helicopter rented by a television station in Des Moines flew in from the southwest and circled the town for a few minutes. Some in the rally were truly frightened and thought they were being targeted again by another ICE raid, so the helicopter was asked to leave, and it did not reappear again during the march to the plant.

There were a number of interesting twists and turns to the anniversary of the raid in Postville. One was that by pure coincidence, the major Jewish holiday of Lag B'Omer fell on May 12, 2009. Lag B'Omer typically occurs thirty-three days following Passover. The actual date of the holiday is different from year to year because of the link between Jewish holidays and solar/lunar calendars. Lag B'Omer is a festive holiday during which people are supposed to leave all of their troubles behind and focus on themes of hope, faith, renewal, and miracles. It is celebrated with special prayers, bonfires, parties, and, in Postville, an annual parade through downtown. Realizing that the Lab B'Omer parade is festive occasion for Jews in Postville, some community leaders immediately became concerned that people would take the joyful nature of the parade on the anniversary of the ICE raid as a sign of disrespect for the detainees and their advocates or even a celebration of the raid. Of course, this was never the intent of the Lag B'Omer organizers in town, and the fact that the parade fell on the morning of the raid anniversary was sheer coincidence.

The parade included several floats, decorated cars, children and adults walking or riding their bikes in formation, and even a small band. A parade permit was acquired and the six blocks from the synagogue to the fair grounds were blocked off by the police in order to divert traffic around the parade route. Large groups of Orthodox Jews from several major Midwestern cities came, and several hundred joined the parade and the parties afterwards.

The parade went on as planned, but there were accommodations to note the raid anniversary. The theme was building community, and several aspects of the parade reflected this. For example, some of the floats featured large signs that read "Positiville," a play on the town's name. Some of the marchers wore hard hats with lettering that read "Community Builder." In typical form, Jewish-upon-Jewish rivalries and disagreements continued, even during the parade. Some of the Orthodox Jews visiting the town from other states carried signs with a photo of Postville that read "Truth Builds Our Community . . . Agendas Destroy It!" In smaller print, various "agendas" were identified in symbols, such as that for People for the Ethical Treatment of Animals (PETA), which represented an earlier flashpoint between Reform and Orthodox Jews related to Agri's controversial slaughtering methods; and *Hechsher Tzedek*, the movement by Reform and Conservative Jews to include treatment of workers as criteria in the kosher certification process. Many Jews in Postville were surprised and disappointed that these signs were inserted into the parade. While they may have agreed with the sentiments of the message in the signs, they felt the signs' insertion into a sacred festival was inappropriate.

With the Lag B'Omer parade gone off without a hitch, Postville turned its attention to the ICE raid service and march in the afternoon of May 12, 2009. Well over 500 people participated in the prayer service and march. In a small town like Postville, even 500 people looks like an army, and the crowd stretched out for nearly three blocks. At every corner there were police or state troopers. The rally was led by the same Christian and Jewish leaders who led the prayer service earlier in the day. They carried a banner that read "Daily through the doors of our house pass some of the most innocent 'criminals' ever created by a failed immigration policy! Cry Out for Reform! Cry Out for Justice!"

When the procession reached the Agri plant property, four nervous Agri staff members—a ragtag security force—stood ready to keep people from entering plant property. A pickup truck was pulled up to the end of the street, and various priests and rabbis climbed on the bed. For some time, many Jews in town questioned why the march would go to Agri. But what happened was yet another example of the kind of accommodations people in Postville make. Instead of condemning Agriprocessors and calling for prosecution of plant leaders, the priests and rabbis "blessed" the plant and its new owner, whoever it might be, and wished it well.

Postville after the ICE raid has set an example of how arbitrary and large-scale enforcement of immigration law can bring a town to its knees. Yet, in many ways the town has pulled together to solve short-term problems and look to the future. One important effort was the formation of the Postville Response Coalition. This coalition was funded by the Methodist and Lutheran churches and private foundations. No government resources were made available, other than two VISTA volunteers provided by the Iowa Civil Rights Commission. In general, government resources were not made available to help Postville rebuild, because it was never declared a disaster area by the state or federal government. By law, those declarations typically can occur only when communities have experienced significant natural catastrophes such as tornadoes and floods, not sudden and massive economic collapse due to immigration raids and bankruptcy of primary employers due to charges of illegal activities. Even local chapters of the Red Cross declined to help the town of Postville after the raid for identical reasons.

The Response Coalition set up an office downtown where resources and referrals were made available to established and newcomer residents. An informal and sometimes contentious division of labor developed between the Response Coalition and St. Bridget's: the Catholic church would take care of the families directly impacted by the raid and the material witnesses while the Response Coalition would take of other newcomers and established residents in need of assistance. The response team also set up Camp Noah for the summer of 2009, a therapeutic leisure program designed for children who have gone through traumatic disasters.

The Response Coalition also nominally coordinated efforts to plan for Postville's future. Two efforts were underway. The first involved "visioning" and planning for a "Long-Term Community Recovery Strategy" facilitated by a professor at the University of Iowa. The second effort included Jewish Community Action and the Jewish Council of Urban Affairs. Working the local churches, the city, the Response Coalition and others, these Jewish groups sought to prepare a Community Benefits Agreement between the community and the next owner of the Agri plant. Their proposal would be a legally binding agreement between the town and the new company to assure fair treatment of workers, living wages for employees, social stability, and corporate contributions to help support the multiple costs associated with assisting newcomers in town. Preparing such an agreement was a timely and understandable reaction to the reality of the aftermath of the raid and the disturbing criminal charges assessed against Agri's plant owners. Unfortunately, as of June 2009, the Community Benefits Agreement remains an idealist contract still waiting to be signed, because it presumes that there would be a new owner of the plant one day and that its managers would agree to abide by Postville's new demands for corporate responsibility. Both of these are only presumptions at this point, because the plant remains under the management of the back bankruptcy trustees and has yet to transfer to new formal ownership.

# CHAPTER NINE

# Lessons Learned in Surviving Diversity

**P**OSTVILLE'S EXPERIMENT IN DIVERSITY worked well for so many years because of its emphasis on accommodation. To those who work in the immigration field, accommodation is the opposite of assimilation. Accommodation means coexisting in a state of mutual respect and tolerance. It means that neither newcomers nor established residents need to change their cultural or religious beliefs and practices as long as the broader community isn't affected negatively by them. It's the social equivalent of the medical doctor's Hippocratic oath: "First, do no harm."

Accommodation is the subtle nod at the local grocery store that says, "We know each other well enough to let each live our own life." It's also an unspoken agreement to be there for each other when needed.

When the satellite trucks rolled out of Postville and the reporters had filed their stories, people got back to the mundane work of living their lives—the little headaches; the small rewards; the inspiration of the human spirit that expresses itself in getting the kids to school on time, buying the groceries, and preparing for the Sabbath, whether Christian or Jew.

Postville has seen its share of conflict and misunderstandings. It's faced ugly times, such as those during and after the ICE raid. But the town also has had its share of simple, day-to-day triumphs of human dignity. Left to their own devices, the various populations in Postville learned how to make things work no matter how awkward those workings might seem to outsiders. The various ethnic communities in Postville have tended to leave each other in peace to follow their own traditions and cultural practices. At key times, both in celebrations and emergencies, the groups have come together. Individuals from every group have formed close relationships—Christians with Jews, Latinos with whites—even if there have been no utopian group moments. Whatever their background, the people of Postville always are a practical people; theirs has been a marriage of convenience in the real world. Day-to-day life in Postville—or anywhere else—is rarely as inspiring as the world might like it to be. Expectations for Postville were always unrealistic; the town never was and never could be a multicultural paradise.

The problem with expectations is what to do when they go unmet. Those who expected Postville to provide answers, to furnish some sort of universal inspiration for humanity, have been frustrated.

People imposed their own standards of success and failure on Postville. Many outsiders—individuals, organizations, and some in the media—believed they had the right to make Postville what they wanted it to be, to put their own stamp on the community. As we noted earlier, some outsiders imposed their own language on the town—both the politically correct rhetoric of the corporate diversity industry and the hate-mongering terms of racists and xenophobes. Many remained mired in their own feelings and experiences while interacting with the community.

Countless people looked to Postville for answers. Countless others expected the community to fail and waited to say "I told you so." To this latter group, Postville was a flash in the pan, soon to become another failed experiment in multiculturalism.

We are here to say that Postville hasn't failed. Nor has it met the unrealistic expectations of the politically correct diversity crowd. There is no one lesson to be learned from Postville's experiment in multiculturalism. Neither is there just one reason why the community has had such a horrible experience in the year after the raid. By our count, there are at least nine major factors that played into the current downfall of Postville, but these factors can serve as lessons to help rebuild the community as well. The lessons that Postville has learned should be heeded by other small towns as well in rural America that are experiencing rapid ethnic changes due to globalization, human migration, and a new world economy.

*Lesson 1: The primary employers and organizations serving newcomers in rural communities must adhere to the highest ethical, legal, and humane standards of operations.*

The criminal activities and allegations swirling around Postville's largest employer, Agriprocessors, are staggering for a privately owned business. Postville's plant was neither the first nor the last meatpacking company raided by ICE. But it is one of only a very few where so much legal attention has been laid upon the owners and managers. They were arrested and some found guilty on hundreds and even thousands of serious criminal charges, many relating to employee hiring and treatment. The arrests of managers crippled the plant, which is millions of dollars in debt and has yet to regain a fraction of its former operating power. The post-raid period brought chaos to the local community, and the economic effects rippled throughout Iowa and the region. At one point, more than 1,000 local people were employed at Agriprocessors.

If diversity efforts are to succeed, employers who rely on immigrants and other marginalized, vulnerable populations must operate their businesses ethically, legally, and humanely for all staff, including newcomers. These standards for fair and just operations must also apply to for-profit, nonprofit, and governmental support organizations for newcomers in areas such as housing, transportation, and others services.

Few communities—even those with much larger populations and greater resources than Postville—could overcome the enormous legal, economic, and social consequences Postville has faced since the Agri raid. When a town's primary employer is mired in criminal charges, allegations, and legal action, even the best diversity efforts become irrelevant: no one is left to benefit from them, because the irresponsible actions of a major employer can bring down the economy of an entire region around it.

*Lesson 2: The United States requires significant immigration reform that recognizes the new economic realities of globalization, changing demographics, and the need for an international labor pool to keep up with expanded world markets for services and products.*

Postville was a victim of immigration policies that fail to respond to the labor needs of a new global economy. The native population of rural America is dying or moving away. Postville and small towns like it need workers, and there are people that need the jobs they offer. The problem is how to match them up—legally. As things stand, both sides are encouraged to cheat. That's what happened in Postville. The plant needed a workforce, and despite the relatively low wages, people were willing to take the jobs.

Agri implemented a number of illegal and unethical labor practices. By industry standards, its workers were underpaid and underinsured. But many people were desperate enough to risk leaving their homes in places such as Guatemala and come to Postville to work at dangerous, low-paying jobs. The problems arise when employees and employers work under federal immigration policies that are outdated and do not take into account the reality of a new global marketplace. Both sides are tempted to cheat, one by entering and working in the U.S. illegally and the other by hiring workers who are obviously in the country illegally.

The May 2008 ICE raid at Agriprocessors showed how desperately this country needs immigration reform. In Postville, a guest-worker program could have worked. Employers and employees could find each other, arrange a legal relationship, and avoid the abuses that are often heaped on desperate workers who prefer to not draw the attention of immigration officials.

Instead, Postville got the ICE raid, which stripped Agri of half of its workforce and scared off many more workers. The raid also ultimately stripped Postville of 40 percent of its population.

*Lesson 3: For-profit corporations that employ immigrants must provide a greater share of the significant hidden and actual costs that small communities incur for providing social, education, health, security, and related services for these newcomers.*

Rural communities benefit from the presence of large employers such as Agriprocessors. When the plant was functioning at its peak, Postville's tax revenues and payrolls swelled, housing stock filled, livestock sold at a brisk pace, and local businesses turned a profit by selling goods and services to the plant and its employees.

However, the nature of the meatpacking business has changed dramatically since the old Hygrade plant was open in Postville. In those days, meatpacking was a respectable working-class job. But in the 1980s, the industry restructured and new plants began paying much lower wages—about one-third of what their predecessors paid. Many new plants offered inadequate health insurance. Now the costs of maintaining a plant's workforce are passed to the workers and their host communities. Among many other issues, high turnover and transient rates contribute to higher expenditures on law enforcement and growing demand for social support services such as food banks.

In Postville and throughout the nation, local churches, food banks, social service agencies, and individuals have struggled to provide for the financial and human needs of an immigrant workforce. Too many small towns, desperate for new businesses and new jobs, allow employers to set up camp in their community without paying their fair and appropriate share of taxes to support the hidden costs of immigrant employees.

After the ICE raid in Postville, such costs skyrocketed. Many Guatemalan women with children were allowed to stay in Postville, but they weren't allowed to work. The local churches solicited contributions to pay for their rent and utilities. The churches also ramped up the local food bank and helped people apply for government benefits such as heat assistance. Immigrants and refugees weren't the only ones seeking these services. After the plant had been closed for a few months, many Jewish families received food donations from the local kosher market and applied for government rent and utility assistance. And yet, the detainees not imprisoned were dumped back on the community without permission to work, further burdening the town. The need for services points to the hidden costs of corporate irresponsibility in small towns across America. Small towns should enter into positive "community benefit agreements" with large employers before allowing them to begin operations in their communities.

*Lesson 4: In their economic development efforts, small communities should recognize that it is important to manage the speed at which diverse populations must be absorbed into a community in order to mitigate resettlement challenges for service providers.*

We contend that Postville has done remarkably well in the face of overwhelming challenges. But it has struggled mightily to absorb the enormous influx of newcomers and the near-constant shifts in its population. It is a living example of what "rapid" ethnic diversification looks like in a small community. Large cities can assimilate vast numbers of people of different ethnicities, national origins, and classes with relative speed. Some are legal immigrants; some are not. It's been going on for generations. But in a town as tiny as Postville (pop. 2,000), immigrant assimilation is a different story, and the sudden and rapid influx of newcomers can be particularly difficult.

Over the past decade, people from at least fifty countries, speaking at least forty languages, have called Postville their home. Many others have come from within the U.S., including ex-convicts and re-covering drug addicts. Most arrived with little notice but in large numbers in a relatively short amount of time.

Postville, Northeast Iowa, and many other rural places can be overwhelmed with trying to provide services to these unique populations in a rapid man-ner. Timely and efficient provision of social services requires thoughtful and costly assessment, prepara-tion, planning, and follow-up, which is difficult to do is the diversification process occurs over a relatively short amount of time. Small communities have too few resources to begin with. They often lack suffi-cient medical and social services and law-enforce-ment personnel, and are poorly suited to respond to sudden and unexpected shifts in their population.

It's remarkable that Postville has been able to meet even a fraction of the needs of newcomers, who often arrive *en masse* from recruiters with no warning. Some other meatpacking towns have federally fund-ed health clinics or professional full-time fire depart-ments or bilingual police officers. These towns tend to thrive better during rapid ethnic diversification. In Postville, despite the dedication of key individuals, there never were—and likely never will be—sufficient resources to meet the needs of a rapidly fluctuating population.

*Lesson 5: Microplurality—small numbers of immigrants from a wide variety of countries— brings with it special needs, concerns, barriers, and expenses that may far exceed those presented by larger minority populations in rural communities.*

The growing phenomenon of "microplurality" in rural America presents many challenges. In small communities, limited resources and services often stretch further with a few large immigrant groups than with numerous smaller ones.

In Postville, Jews and Mexicans were the two largest newcomer populations for many years. Each population numbered in the hundreds. Health-care providers, law enforcement officials, and other services got used to working with these populations; they communicated in Spanish and Hebrew and grew comfortable with their cultures and behaviors. But Postville has also experienced microplurality—an influx of smaller newcomer populations, each ethnically and linguistically distinct.

When all these populations occupy the same community, and one as small as Postville, you have a recipe for confusion, chaos, and conflict. At the time of the Agriprocessors raid, Postville hosted a wildly diverse set of newcomers, including recently released prisoners; people in addiction-recovery programs; Africans from five different countries, including Somalia, Ethiopia, and Kenya; Guatemalan peasants; Palauans; and others. These many microgroups—some containing a dozen or fewer individuals—posed serious challenges for health-care workers, schools, medical staff, law enforcement, and others. It makes sense to hire interpreters when you have 300 Spanish speakers in a community. But what if you have only seven Sudanese who speak Nuer or Dinka? And how can rural towns provide culturally appropriate social services to microgroups that may only be around for two months? The specialized needs of these small groups may be beyond the capacity of rural communities to serve adequately, and require more intensive infusions of funding and resources to address.

*Lesson 6: A community needs multiple champions of diversity and supporters of multiculturalism, as well as their trainees and replacements, to sustain diversity initiatives in the long term.*

We've spent many years studying rural towns with rapidly changing ethnic mixes. Over time, we developed something we call the 20-60-20 rule. In most communities, the established-resident population can be divided into three camps. About 20 percent embrace diversification and believe that the newcomers make their community more interesting and vital. These folks comprise the "choir"; there's no need to convince them that welcoming and accommodating newcomers is a good thing.

Another 20 percent are convinced that diversification of the community is a bad thing. For whatever reason—ethnocentrism, racism, even anti-Semitism—there's no convincing these people to reconsider their perspectives. Many confess that given the choice between letting their community die with a dwindling population or thrive with newcomers, they'd choose the former.

Between the choir and the impossible-to-convince camps are the other 60 percent. These are people who aren't sure what to think about diversification. They're generally open to learning more about it, and about the newcomers themselves, but they don't know what questions to ask. Many of these people could go either way: toward rejecting of newcomers and favoring their departure or toward finding accord with them.

The 20-60-20 rule holds true in any size community. Obviously, the larger the community is, the more likely it is to have a greater number of people in each group. Large communities can count a good number of choir members. These are the people who volunteer to tutor English learners and help people find housing, get their kids registered for school, and help immigrants apply for drivers' licenses. They advocate for newcomers. They speak positively about what newcomers bring to their community.

But in a tiny place like Postville, that same 20 percent represents a minuscule number of people—perhaps fewer than fifty. That's simply not enough people to meet all the town's advocacy and service needs. Fortunately, the choir's efforts were supplemented by outsiders.

Still, small towns such as Postville can't rely forever on a relative handful of tolerant, pro-diversity people. Eventually these individuals will burn out or move away, and there won't be any back-ups ready to step in and pick up the diversity ball. With some notable and very worthy exceptions such as Merle Turner and others, the people who made and kept a long-term commitment to Postville's diversity challenges did so as part of their professional or vocational activities. Volunteers bring energy and a genuine desire to make things better, but they can't be expected to do so indefinitely.

*Lesson 7: Common sense and a broader, more realistic understanding of cultural diversity must replace political correctness, which often stifles more meaningful communication and appropriate actions.*

America's obsession with political correctness has made many people afraid to express their feelings and has led to less, rather than more, communication among diverse populations. For example, so many non-Jews in Postville were afraid of being accused of anti-Semitism that they backed away from calling some of the Jews on their behavior. Here are two examples: Years ago, when Jews parked their cars illegally, the Postville police were reluctant to give out tickets because they might be accused of anti-Jewish bias. Likewise, many non-Jewish service providers and business owners were afraid to push Jews for payment of overdue bills.

Similar stories could be told about whites, Latinos, and Africans in Postville. Our point is that people should treat each other with respect, and express legitimate concerns through respectful dialogue when they need to. That includes recognizing people as individuals with responsibilities and obligations to the larger community, and not just dealing with them as members of their own ethnic group. Even if one culture does not fully assimilate or integrate into the existing larger culture, both sides should function in an air of accommodation. In other words, groups must learn to exist side by side with respect and tolerance for each other, even if they do not fully interact with each other. Individuals of all backgrounds must strive to obey the broader rules and regulations established for the betterment and well-being of the community as a whole, while maintaining their own unique historical and cultural identities. It *is* possible to do both. In politically correct America, though, people have been made to feel so afraid of offending one another they have forgotten how to have an honest conversation about the needs and concerns of the community as a whole.

*Lesson 8: Successful integration and accommodation of newcomers in small towns ultimately requires the involvement of all sectors of the community, including the immigrants themselves, the local residents, the private and nonprofit sectors, and the government at the local, state, and national levels.*

When communities go into crisis after natural disasters such as floods or tornadoes, the government steps in to coordinate relief efforts. Political and other leaders are on site within a day or two, promising funding and mobilization of resources. It's the humane—and politically astute—thing to do. But where is the response to human and economic disasters? After the ICE raid in Postville, government officials and local politicians remained silent, mostly because they wouldn't touch the immigration controversy with a barge pole. The lack of a formal and coordinated response from local, county, and state leaders was astonishing. Only a tiny number of state and federal officials came to Postville to see the community, and they did not do so until months after the raid. As we mentioned earlier, during the period when unemployed Palauans and African Americans were being evicted and the food bank couldn't keep up with demand, the local mayor was away on a hunting trip in Colorado, so several groups and individuals stepped in to help provide urgently needed assistance. The manager of Radio Postville, Jeff Abbas, and a handful of dedicated volunteers turned the station into a shelter and soup kitchen for displaced newcomers. Filling a void, the Catholic church in Postville also helped the detained Guatemalan population and, working with the other churches in town, kept the food bank stocked and teeming with volunteers.

In sum, all elements of a society must pull together during times of disaster and crisis. This includes local, state, county, and federal government agencies, as well as the non-profit and for-profit sectors as well. The individuals affected most directly by a crisis must be empowered and provided support that develops their ability to take charge of their own futures eventually so that they do not require ongoing, costly assistance. It is worth noting, too, that relief and response efforts should be broad based, inclusive, and comprehensive. If they are too narrow and not integrated into larger efforts, these aid strategies can sometimes have unintended consequences where one constituency benefits at the expense of another. This happened briefly when some of the Guatemalan women detainees formed themselves into a weaver's guild after the raid. They went on the road to local communities and talked about their experiences to sympathetic audiences. They were able to raise some funds for their cause while displaying their beautiful, intricately woven products to the public and participating in these presentations. However, some other Guatemalan women back in Postville soon complained to local relief workers that they resented the attention (and money) the weavers were receiving, and the situation caused an unfortunate but temporary rift in relationships with each other among the Guatemalans.

*Lesson 9: Citizens must become more educated about their role in the global economy and understand that their desire for cheap foods and goods drives the need for inexpensive international laborers.*

We, the consumers, also play a role in Postville's ongoing struggle with diversity in the new global economy. The Agri plant produced both kosher and non-kosher products. All consumers benefit from relatively low food costs—costs that are borne on the backs of poorly paid and often vulnerable populations, from migrant workers in the Central Valley of California to Guatemalans at the Postville meat plant. Our globalized and integrated food systems have separated consumers from producers so thoroughly that we disregard the role of labor in food production. Most people consider only the end point: product availability and price. They do not think about larger issues such as immigration or mismanaged diversity initiatives or the social consequences of migration to rural communities.

When consumers are forced to confront these issues—when, for example, ICE raids a packing plant that produces the meat they consume—most still try to avoid acknowledging *their* role in a dysfunctional system. It's infinitely easier and more convenient to blame illegal immigrants and the meatpacking companies. Consumers want simple solutions and scapegoats. They don't want to be reminded that they, too, are culpable in today's intertwined global market.

So Postville continues with its struggle for diversity. Some of these problems can be addressed at the micro or local level, while others require greater federal involvement. The answers are not easy, and there is not a single solution that will fix the debacle that is now consuming Postville. The strategies and solutions must be ongoing, comprehensive, and multipronged. As noted in the lessons above, corporations that need immigrant labor must help contribute to the very real infrastructure costs of meeting the needs of these workers from health, education, law enforcement, and related areas. Relief and support services for newcomers must be coordinated at the local, county, and state levels, because individual volunteers and nonprofit agencies can't be expected to meet immigrant needs over the long haul.

The migrants themselves also have to take an active and responsible role in their new communities, making every effort to learn the local language and respect the local culture. Locals should provide acculturation resources to help immigrants achieve this difficult transition. Both sides have a responsibility to behave ethically and contribute to the common good of the community. Likewise, all individuals must strive to be culturally sensitivity and more tolerant of others in their midst.

Over the years, many people have attempted to make Postville what they wanted it to be. But as we noted earlier, it's time to get past the talk about diversity, and stop asking whether one community's diversity is more legitimate than another's. It's time to also get past "valuing diversity" as a dodge when people don't want to talk about difficult issues such as class, or acknowledge their own political agendas. With the new demographic reality in the United States that is spreading even to rural America, it is well past time that we start acting in earnestness to achieve multicultural communities that work, because they are so clearly here to stay.

If Postville has one central lesson to teach, it's that accommodation among diverse populations does take a lot of work, but people can and do make it happen—when allowed to do so on their own terms. Postville had momentum to do just that, but it was temporarily disrupted by the ICE raid and the corporate crimes it exposed at the town's major employer.

Postville has the seeds for its revitalization—they just need to be sown. The town's long-term economic prospects rely on the success of the Agri plant. The plant clearly needs new managers who will run it competently and ethically. This—we hope—will mean higher wages and health benefits for all workers. Because of the recent economic downturn, more local Iowans might even seek work at the plant as well.

The seeds of revitalization, rebirth, and survival in Postville can best be seen in the incredible volunteer spirit that came out again after the ICE raid. Individuals of all ethnicities prepared meals for the detainees and those who lost their homes; they brought supplies to the food pantry and helped keep it running; and they helped pay rent and utilities for those who couldn't work. There are too many unsung heroes to list, but they did what they needed as community members when Postville was gasping for breath. For example, we recognize the work of people like Mordy Brown, a Jewish immigrant and manager of the kosher grocery store, who, without pay, kept the grocery open and made sure there was enough kosher food in town. Donations from synagogues in other

communities helped make this possible. We also recognize people like Lyle Opheim, a local Christian
businessman who kept many Agri workers employed
by paying Agri's overdue utility bill so the plant could
keep running at least part time. There are so many
Mordys and Lyles in Postville, and more are waiting
to emerge. They simply need the encouragement and
resources to step forward and succeed.

Ultimately, the tragedy of Postville and its future
destiny will rest on significant immigration reform.
In the bigger picture, this country must enact significant changes in these policies, and soon. We urgently need a legal immigrant workforce because of our
own shrinking labor pool. This workforce should be
protected from unscrupulous business owners who
exploit them in the name of profit and expediency.
Consumers must also start taking responsibility for
their role in the global economic system and advocate for fair trade that pays workers living wages
commensurate with their labor. The Obama administration offers strong prospects for new legislation
that will simultaneously protect the human rights of
migrant workers but will allow businesses to find the
laborers they so desperately need. An obscure little
town in Northeast Iowa suffered mightily under this
country's outdated and failed immigration policies,
and "No More Postvilles!" could be a powerful slogan
for reform.

We remain optimistic that Postville can rebound
and ultimately serve as a model to other rural communities facing the promise and challenges of diversity in a new America. Most importantly, the people

of Postville appear to be optimistic as well. These are tough people who get through tough times. They want their town to be remembered as more than just the place where a community collapsed after the nation's largest immigration raid at the time. The resiliency and fortitude of Postvillians of all ethnicities today can best be demonstrated by the actions of some members of the community who draped a large banner over the Agriprocessors water tower recently. It read simply, "Postville: Hometown of Hope."

# AN AFTERWORD

DESPITE THE STORM of emotions surrounding Postville after the ICE raid and the intense feelings we share, we've attempted to write a balanced account of what happened. Apparently, it was too balanced for some. One East Coast book agent declined to represent our book because it was "too straightforward." He wanted more "character development." But the multicultural residents of Postville are not "characters." They are real people. We weren't all that surprised by the book agent's reaction. Most of what has been written and said about Postville has been more about personalities and oddities, rather than about the daily bump and grind of making diverse communities work. Character development is all well and good—and Postville certainly has its share of interesting characters like anywhere else—but this book is not about individuals. It's about a community.

An Orthodox rabbi in Des Moines made an interesting observation about this situation. He described the difference between the substance of Postville and the debate this way: "When it comes to Postville, most people have sold the sizzle, not the steak."

⇒·⇐

With this in mind, we can anticipate the responses and questions to our book from several quarters. Some will feel that we did not come down hard enough on Agriprocessor's management for their business practices. The reason is simple: this book was written and published before any of Shalom Rubashkin's trials have been held on the array of charges he faces. The legal process is moving along so slowly that frankly it might be another year or two before any decisions by juries have been returned against him.

Postville is more than just a raid, after all, and this book is about the broader struggle for diversity in Postville. It is not a treatise on the Rubashkins or Agriprocessors.

Several Agri managers have already plead guilty to federal charges. Some were already sentenced. The former supervisor of the beef-line received a three-year prison sentence for conspiring to hire illegal immigrants, as well as aiding and abetting their hiring. Rubashkin's attorneys are trying to get his own charges dismissed or split up for separate trials, and they hope to move the trial(s) outside Iowa. As evidence that an unbiased jury could not be seated in Iowa, Rubashkin and his co-defendants submitted hundreds of newspaper articles, recordings of radio programs, and Bloom's *Postville* book to show the extensive coverage of the case locally. Interestingly, the federal judge denied this request for a change in venue, noting, "The role and influence of the printed newspaper in society is not the same as it was a generation ago. Similarly, the court does not know how widely read *Postville* is among prospective jurors. The book predates the trial by the better part of a decade, although it is apparently still in print." The judge did leave open the possibility of a change of venue after the jury selection process was under way.

Rubashkin is within his rights to ask for all of these things, although one of his attorneys was out of line when he equated Iowa with "Nazi-occupied Poland." Especially for those of us who have visited or had family members affected by the death camps, it was deeply insulting to suggest Iowa is capable of hosting concentration camps and gas chambers.

After reading this book, people may also react by questioning why the management of Agriprocessors was impacted so heavily by the raid, which ultimately, after all, caused the collapse of the company and the near-bankruptcy of the town. It is a question we get quite often, from Jews and non-Jews alike: since hiring illegal immigrants is said to be pervasive in the meatpacking industry, and ICE has raided several other packing plants over the years, why were Rubashkin and his managers indicted when most other managers were not?

Many Jews, when asked, suspect the Agri plant got special attention because the owners were Jewish, but the real answer may be more complicated. First, major meatpacking plants in this country are owned and operated by huge corporations. The plant managers are parts of massive bureaucracies, and the first rule of any bureaucracy is to protect itself. Distribute responsibility among many actors and in the end, no single individual takes the blame. The history of federal prosecution against large packing plants has been replete with attempts to convict individuals working in massive bureaucracies where responsibility usually can be dispersed among numerous people and along bureaucratic processes. It becomes it is very difficult to convict individuals who are seen as just cogs in a giant machine.

Agri was different from the big packers for one important reason: it was owned and operated by a single family. There was no large bureaucracy, no system in which individuals could hide, and no way to disperse responsibility. Even at Agri, no individual could have known what was going on at all times. But Shalom Rubashkin was the boss, so he ultimately was responsible for everything that transpired.

With the arrests and indictments that followed the ICE raid, it's reasonable to ask how much Rubashkin *did* know about his employees' alleged activities. If some of his managers were involved in illegal or unethical activities—and clearly some confessed to crimes or fled the country after charges were leveled—why didn't Rubashkin do anything about it? Why weren't they fired?

We don't know because the trials against Shalom have yet to occur, although theories, rumors, and gossip abound in town, the media, and the blogosphere.

Agri may have received more legal scrutiny than other plants simply because, as a privately owned, family-operated business, it was more transparent.

This raises another question: How did Rubashkin allow his family and plant to become so vulnerable to a federal investigation in the first place?

Aaron feels that the Rubashkins appear to be, plain and simple, a family of butchers with expertise in producing kosher and non-kosher meat and marketing those products to a wide variety of buyers. As the plant grew and its production and markets expanded, the Rubashkins lost touch with their roots. In essence, the business outgrew them, and they lost control of their message and their oversight. In other words, they were lousy at public relations and management.

But the picture is a bit murkier. Allegedly, Shalom was concerned enough about the possibility of criminal charges that he destroyed evidence when he was released on bail following the raid. He also allegedly engaged in money laundering to pay illegal workers in cash through a local evangelical church, which could presumably indicate previous knowledge of the criminal nature of the activity.

As problems grew at the plant, the Rubashkins did nothing to stanch the damage. Could things have turned out differently if they had acted differently— or acted at all? Why not get rid of the problem managers before they became a liability? Downstream, public relations and the ability to thwart federal and state interest in the plant could not be handled by media spin.

After the feds handed down their initial indictments, Shalom Rubashkin was held in custody for a few days. When he was released, there was a party in the Postville *shul*. It is traditional for Jews to host a thanksgiving celebration after someone is released from jail. That was the intent of the Postville party; it wasn't a political statement. But the party was videotaped, and it ended up on the Internet.

Most members of the Postville Jewish community were angry that the party was taped and incensed that the video was posted on the Internet. It was a public relations nightmare, unleashing a storm of condemnation. Outsiders felt that given Rubashkin's serious legal situation, he should have humbled himself, laid low, and not flaunted his freedom. Rubashkin apparently never considered the party's potential for negative publicity. He seemed to remain naïve or to lack understanding about how exposed he could be to critics and law enforcement officials. In the age of the Internet and cell phone video cameras, there are no secrets.

When more federal indictments were handed down and Rubashkin was detained for a second time—this one much longer than the first—he was initially denied bail because the U.S. Attorney convinced the judge that he was a flight risk. Large sums of money were found in his home. Prosecutors also noted Israel's "Right of Return" policy, which grants entry to any Jew who wishes to live in the country. Prosecutors argued Rubashkin would use the "Right of Return" to move to Israel, where it would be difficult or impossible to bring him to justice.

Jews in Chabad and elsewhere felt this amounted to anti-Semitism, since Rubashkin was denied bail based on a policy limited to Jews. After visiting Rubashkin in jail, a group of Orthodox rabbis held a press conference condemning use of the "Right of Return" policy to deny Rubashkin bail.

Eventually, Rubashkin's attorneys convinced a second judge that citing the "Right of Return" policy to deny bail amounted to discrimination. Rubashkin was granted bail after he agreed to forfeit his and his wife's passports, to wear an ankle GPS tracking unit, to remain in Allamakee County, and to have no contact with people involved in the case. He apparently learned his lesson from the party-in-the-*shul* debacle. He threw no more celebrations, maintained a low profile, had no contact with press, and gave critics nothing to broadcast on the Internet.

Unfortunately, the Internet and the blogosphere encourage speculation, in no small part because people can post opinions and rumors anonymously. We all notice how much time Postville residents spend trying to figure out who are the people in town contributing to various websites using aliases such as "Hometown Postville," State of Postville," "Curious Postville Native," or "Concerned for the Postville Area."

❧❧

We can also anticipate the response to this book from people in the diversity business and those who will charge us with a lack of political correctness.

Some will attack our cynicism about the diversity industry by calling us out of touch or biased. They may suggest our work and perspectives on diversity, ethnic and religious relations, and Postville are subjective and narrowly framed by our own experience and ethnic and religious backgrounds. Our response is that all perspectives on important issues, including ethnic relations, are subjective. Anyone, regardless of ethnicity or religion, is capable of bias.

We've tried to be upfront about who are and how we approached this book. We are professional observers of the human condition, and we've worked successfully with multiple cultures and ethnic and religious groups. We have our personal and professional perspectives, but we've attempted, as much as possible, to leave behind our own biases and present a balanced view of Postville and the human and economic tragedy it suffered.

We can also anticipate some pushback about the difficulties of making multiethnic communities work. Making towns like Postville work is *hard work*. Diversity is not all sunshine and roses. Yet, as we emphasize, the work is necessary and rewarding. Given the dramatic shifts in our nation's demographic profile, it's imperative that we do the hard work of making diverse communities work.

※

Some will disagree with our contention that everyone in Postville was a victim of Agri's fall, including Jews, non-Jews, Latinos, and all the other workers, from myriad ethnic groups, who lost their jobs, incomes, and homes. Critics may say we should have put more emphasis on one group and less on others. They may contend that there are degrees of victimhood, and we got the scale wrong.

We disagree. We acknowledged that the workers arrested and convicted in the ICE raid suffered disproportionately. These individuals, ripped from their families and imprisoned for five months, were victims of the government's decision to criminalize their presence in the U.S. They received the lion's share of attention in the media, and rightly so.

But in this book we make the point that there were other victims in Postville, too: the rural Iowan cattle farmers who lost the primary market for their livestock; the Jewish *shochtim* who lost their incomes but had families to feed and mortgages to pay; the Latino store owners forced to shut down their businesses after the Hispanic exodus; the local white plumbers who never got paid after the housing companies lost renters and revenues; the residential taxpayers forced to pay higher water bills to make up for lost revenue after Postville's significant loss of population; and many others. Unfortunately, the multicultural nature of Postville meant that all ethnic groups in town were affected by the raid, but in different ways, at different times, and to different levels.

Earlier we noted Neo-Nazi and white supremacist groups' interest in Postville. No doubt some members of these groups will read our book, pull out a few quotes, take them out of context, and use them to say, "We told you so." The same may be true of others who believe ethnic diversity is bad news for our communities and our society.

We have a clear, unequivocal message for such people: Don't use our honest and forthright depiction of the challenges diverse communities face as an argument that diverse communities are inherently bad. They're not. They can work and must work in order to assure the future of our society. We firmly believe in them and support them.

The notion that the United States should be anything but a diverse and heterogeneous society denies reality and ignores the very principles that make this country great. The U.S. has always been a diverse nation, made up of untold numbers of ethnic and religious groups who believed in the concept of America and committed themselves to a greater good.

Some things are difficult. That doesn't mean they can't or shouldn't happen. If our country is to remain great, we need to make diverse communities work. Nativists and white supremacists may try to convince their neighbors that nonwhite, non-English-speaking, or non-Christian newcomers will lead our society to its demise, but that train left the station a long time ago.

Members of the media may take exception to some of our observations. We respect that media professionals are often under impossible deadlines and face intense competition in a market with fewer and fewer viable outlets for news. An experienced and respected journalist friend said, "Honestly, most reporters aren't out to sensationalize a story. Too often, when the media gets it wrong, it's because the reporters talked to the wrong people. They don't have the luxury of hanging around for months to absorb all this themselves. Walter Lippmann described the press as a roving spotlight, highlighting different events in turn, not a constant floodlight illuminating the entire landscape." Fair enough. That's one of the reasons we wrote this book: to provide a more nuanced perspective, based on years of observation, on the complex landscape of Postville.

⇾⋯⇽

Finally, we anticipate the reaction of our friends and neighbors in Postville. One friend, who was born in Postville and has lived there his entire life, made an observation during the height of the post-raid turmoil in town. When people came and went by the carload, when apartments began to empty and lines at the food bank grew longer, he said, "We'll be OK . . . . Postville will get though this, too." His remarks reflect an upper Midwestern, German-Scandinavian stoicism, one that stubbornly clings to a can-do attitude toward life no matter what troubles it may bring. "This too shall pass," as one Postville native used to say.

We trust that Postvillians who read this book will see our efforts to bring a balanced perspective to the community. Postville is extraordinary for what it has endured. It is also remarkable for what it has to teach the rest of our society about the struggle for diversity.

# GLOSSARY
# OF SPECIAL TERMS

*Ashkenazi*   Jews of European descent.

*Chabad-Lubavitch*   One of the largest movements in Orthodox Judaism, based in the Brooklyn, New York, neighborhood of Crown Heights. Chabad is a Hebrew acronym for *Chochmah, Binah, Da'at,* meaning Wisdom, Understanding, and Knowledge. Chabad-Lubavitch is named after the Russian town *Lyubavichi,* where the movement began in the late eighteenth century.

*cholent*   A Yiddish word for a traditional Jewish stew. The term is often used by Jews to describe a mixture of people in a single community or any other eclectic combination.

*glatt*   A Yiddish term that means *smooth. Glatt* refers to the highest standards of kosher beef, taken from cattle with lungs that are smooth and without holes or other flaws.

*goyim*   A Hebrew word that means *nations*. The term is used by Jews for Gentiles or non-Jews. The singular is *goy*.

*Hassidic*   A term for Orthodox Jews, based on the Hebrew word for *pious*. Orthodox Judaism is often referred to as Hassidism. Members of the Hassidic movement are sometimes referred to as Hassid.

*Kabbalah*   A Hebrew term that means *receiving*. Kabbalah is the discipline and thought associated with Jewish mysticism.

*Kaddish*   From the Aramaic word for *holy*. *Kaddish* refers to central parts of the Jewish prayer service. The *Mourner's Kaddish* is said at funerals and memorials and up to eleven months after the death.

*kashrut*   Jewish dietary laws, including the production of food under *Halakha* (Jewish law).

*kosher*   Food produced, cooked, and served under the laws of *Kashrut*.

*la migra*   A Mexican slang term for U.S. immigration officials.

*Lubavitcher*   A member of the *Chabad-Lubavitch* movement.

*menudo*   Tripe soup. The term is often used by Mexicans and others to describe a mixture of different ethnicities and languages in the same community.

*mikvah*   A bath used for ritual immersion in Judaism. It is used by women after menstruation or childbirth and by men for purification. A Mikvah ceremony is also used when people convert to Judaism.

*pogrom*    From the Russian word meaning *to destroy* or *to wreak havoc*. Jews use the term to describe riots directed towards Jewish communities while police and other officials stand by and allow it to happen.

*Sephardic*    Jews who descend from the Iberian Peninsula. The term also generally includes Jews from Arab countries like Morocco and Yemen.

*shechita*    Ritual slaughter of animals according to Jewish dietary laws.

*shochet*    A ritual slaughterer of animals under the laws of *kashrut*. A *shochet* must be a pious Jew. Most receive specialized training on *shechita*, and they are often ordained rabbis. The plural is *shochtim*.

*shtetl*    A Yiddish term that means *little town*. A shtetl was a small town with a large Jewish population in pre-Holocaust Central and Eastern Europe. The term is often used by Jews as a metaphor for a warm, comforting place.

*Shul*    A Jewish house of worship, sometimes referred to as a synagogue or temple.

*yeshiva*    A rabbinical school where students study Jewish laws and tradition in the Torah, the Talmud, and the Rabbinic literature.

# BIBLIOGRAPHY

Avraham, Hadar. "Victory in Postville." *The Jewish Press*, 4 May 2001.

Bloom, Stephen G. *Postville: A Clash of Cultures in Heartland America*. New York: Harcourt, Inc., 2000.

Bloom, Stephen G. "Hello, I Must be Going: A Midlist Author's Fling with Fame." *The Chronicle Review*, 14 September 2001.

Camayd-Freixas, Erik. "Interpreting after the Largest ICE Raid in U.S. History: A Personal Account." *Monthly Review*, 7 December 2008.

Cable News Network (CNN). "Mayor: Feds Turned my Town 'Topsy Turvy.'" 14 October 2008.

Eisenberg, Robert. *Boychiks in the Hood: Travels In the Hasidic Underground*. New York: Harper Collins, 1995.

Feinstein, Norman, Michele Yehieli, and Mark A. Grey. *Orthodox Jewish Patients in Hospital Settings: A Health Provider's Pocket Guide*. University of Northern Iowa: Iowa EXPORT Center of Excellence on Health Disparities and The New Iowans Program, 2004.

Ford, Anne. "Kosher Meat Shortage Pinches Budgets, Menus." *The Chicago Tribune*, 18 December 2008.

Grey, Mark A. "Book review: *Postville: A Clash of Cultures in Heartland America*." *The Annals of Iowa*, Fall 2002.

Grey, Mark A. "State and Local Immigration Policy in Iowa." Immigration's New Frontiers: Experiences from the Emerging Gateway States. Greg Anrig, Jr., and Tova Andrea Wang, eds. Washington, D.C.: The Century Foundation, 2006.

Hansen, Fay. "Diversity's Business Case Doesn't Add Up." *Workforce*, April 2003.

Iowa Public Television. "Postville: When Cultures Collide." 2001.

Kay, Sara. "Postville Revisited." *New Voices National Jewish Student Magazine*, 24 September 2008.

Kiener, Ronald G. "The Postville Raid." *Religion in the News*, Fall 2008.

Kochan, Thomas A. et al. "The Effects of Diversity on Business Performance: Report of the Diversity Research Network." *Human Resource Management*, Spring 2003.

Krogstad, Jens Manuel. "A year after Agriprocessors raid, Postville still struggles." *Waterloo-Cedar Falls Courier*, 10 May 2009.

Krogstad, Jens Manuel. "Postville on the brink of collapse, town leaders tell Braley." *Waterloo-Cedar Falls Courier*, 30 January 2009.

Lehmann, Chris. "Hasids and Hawkeyes." *The Washington Post*, 15 October 2000.

Leys, Tony. "Hope at Any Cost." *Des Moines Register*, 30 November 2008.

Longworth, Richard. *Caught in the Middle: America's Heartland in the Age of Globalism*. New York: Bloomsbury U.S.A., 2007.

Love, Orlan. "Postville decimated by immigration raid one year ago." *Cedar Rapids Gazette*, 10 May 2009.

Love, Orlan. "Jewish people in Postville threatened—Disgruntled worker vents to radio station; interview hits Internet." *Cedar Rapids Gazette*, 21 November 2008.

Love, Orlan. "Immigration Raid Costs Taxpayers $6.1 Million." *Cedar Rapids Gazette*, 15 October 2008.

Love, Orlan. "Goldsmith Elected to Postville Council." *Cedar Rapids Gazette*, 25 April 2001.

Moyers, Peter R. "Butchering Statutes: The Postville Raid and the Misinterpretation of Federal Criminal Law." *Seattle University Law Review* 32, 3 April 2009.

Nardini, Jennifer. "Postville's Melting Pot Simmers." *Waterloo-Cedar Falls Courier*, 1 April 2001.

Nardini, Jennifer. "Jew Wins Postville Special Election." *Waterloo-Cedar Falls Courier*, 25 April 2001.

Northam, Jackie. "Orthodox Jews in Rural America." National Public Radio, 7 December 1998. http://www.npr.org/templates/story/story.php?storyId=1023695.

Petroski, William. "Tax Payers' Costs Top $5 Million for May Raid at Postville." *Des Moines Register*, 14 October 2008.

Popper, Nathanial. "In Iowa Meat Plant, Kosher 'Jungle' Breeds Fear, Injury, Short Pay." *The Jewish Daily Forward*, 26 May 2006.

Popper, Nathanial. "Agriprocessors Bankruptcy Leaves Iowa Town Flailing." *The Jewish Daily Forward*, 6 November 2008.

Popper, Nathanial. "How the Rubashkins Changed the Way Jews Eat in America." *The Jewish Daily Forward*, 11 December 2008.

Preston, Julia. "An Interpreter Speaking Up for Migrants." *The New York Times*, 11 July 2008.

Putnam, Robert. "*E Pluribus Unum:* Diversity and Community in the Twenty-first Century—The 2006 Johan Skytte Prize Lecture." *Scandinavian Political Studies* 30 (2): 137–174, 2007.

Simon, Stephanie. "Iowa Town Facing a Dilemma." *Los Angeles Times*, 1 February 2001.

# Bibliography

Yehieli, Michele and Mark A. Grey. "Jews." *Health Matters: A Pocket Guide for Working with Diverse Cultures and Underserved Populations.* Boston: Intercultural Press, 2005.

Yoffe, Emily. "In Postville, Iowa, Kosher is Kosher." *National Geographic*, June 2005.

## MARK A. GREY, Ph.D.

Mark A. Grey, Ph.D., is professor of anthropology at the University of Northern Iowa. He is also the founder and director of the Iowa Center for Immigrant Leadership and Integration (ICILI). ICILI is an award-winning organization that provides consultation, training, and publications to Midwestern communities, churches, organizations, and employers as they deal with the unique challenges and opportunities associated with influxes of immigrant and refugee newcomers. Mark received his Ph.D. in applied anthropology at the University of Colorado-Boulder. He has published extensively in academic journals on immigration in rural communities. He has also published extensively for non-academic audiences. Mark has won numerous awards for his activities, including the One Iowa Award, the Iowa Friends of Civil Rights Award, the Iowa Council for International Understanding Vision Award, the Richard Remington Award for Public Health, the University of Northern Iowa Distinguished Service Award, the Midwest Sociological Society Social Action Award, and the Iowa Regents Award for Faculty Excellence.

## MICHELE DEVLIN, Dr.P.H.

Michele Devlin is professor of public health at the University of Northern Iowa, where she is the recipient of the Richard Remington Award, the Governor's Award, the Iowa Civil Rights Award, and other honors for outstanding teaching, scholarship, and service in the health and human rights field. Michele is director of the Iowa Center on Health Disparities, a model organization funded by the National Institutes of Health to improve health equity for underserved populations. She also directs Cultural Connections, a nonprofit consulting organization at the University of Northern Iowa that provides training for agencies on cultural competency, tolerance, and diversity issues. Michele completed her master's and doctorate degrees in international public health at the University of California at Los Angeles. Her primary areas of specialty include refugee, minority, and immigrant care, as well as cultural competency and health communication with underserved populations. Michele has nearly thirty years of field experience working with public health agencies, nonprofits, corporations, and government organizations, conducting programs both domestically and internationally with refugees, women, children, minorities, the elderly, and other at-risk individuals. She is also the founder and advisor of the award-winning Global Health Corps, a model service-learning program for students in culturally competent patient care.

## AARON GOLDSMITH

Aaron Goldsmith is former City Councilman of Postville, Iowa, and resident of the community since 1998. Aaron has a diverse education background, beginning with his business related degree from Drake University in 1979, followed by a rabbinical degree granted by Yeshiva Tomchei Tmimim in Kfar Chabad, Israel, in 1983. After he was appointed as a councilman to the city of Postville in 2001, he was frequently sought for radio and television interviews and speaking engagements on issues related to multiculturalism and diversity. Aaron was the first Orthodox Jew ever elected to a political office in Iowa.

Aaron is a small business owner. He is President of Transfer Master Products, Inc., a manufacturer of custom hospital beds in Postville, Iowa. The company was founded in 1993 by Aaron and his father, Louis, in Long Beach, California. Aaron moved the company to Postville in 1998. In 2001, he was recognized as the Small Business Administration Small Business Person of the Year for Northeast Iowa. He has received multiple patents for the unique beds that the company produces.

On July 20, 2009, U.S. Bankruptcy Court Judge Paul J. Kilburg approved the sale of Agriprocessors to SHF Industries, a company formed in May 2009 by Canadian plastics manufacturer Hershey Friedman and his son-in-law Daniel Hirsch. Freidman stated his intent to operate the plant as a kosher meat processing facility.